I0698357

This Book Belongs to:

____

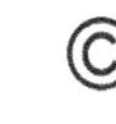

Test Color Page

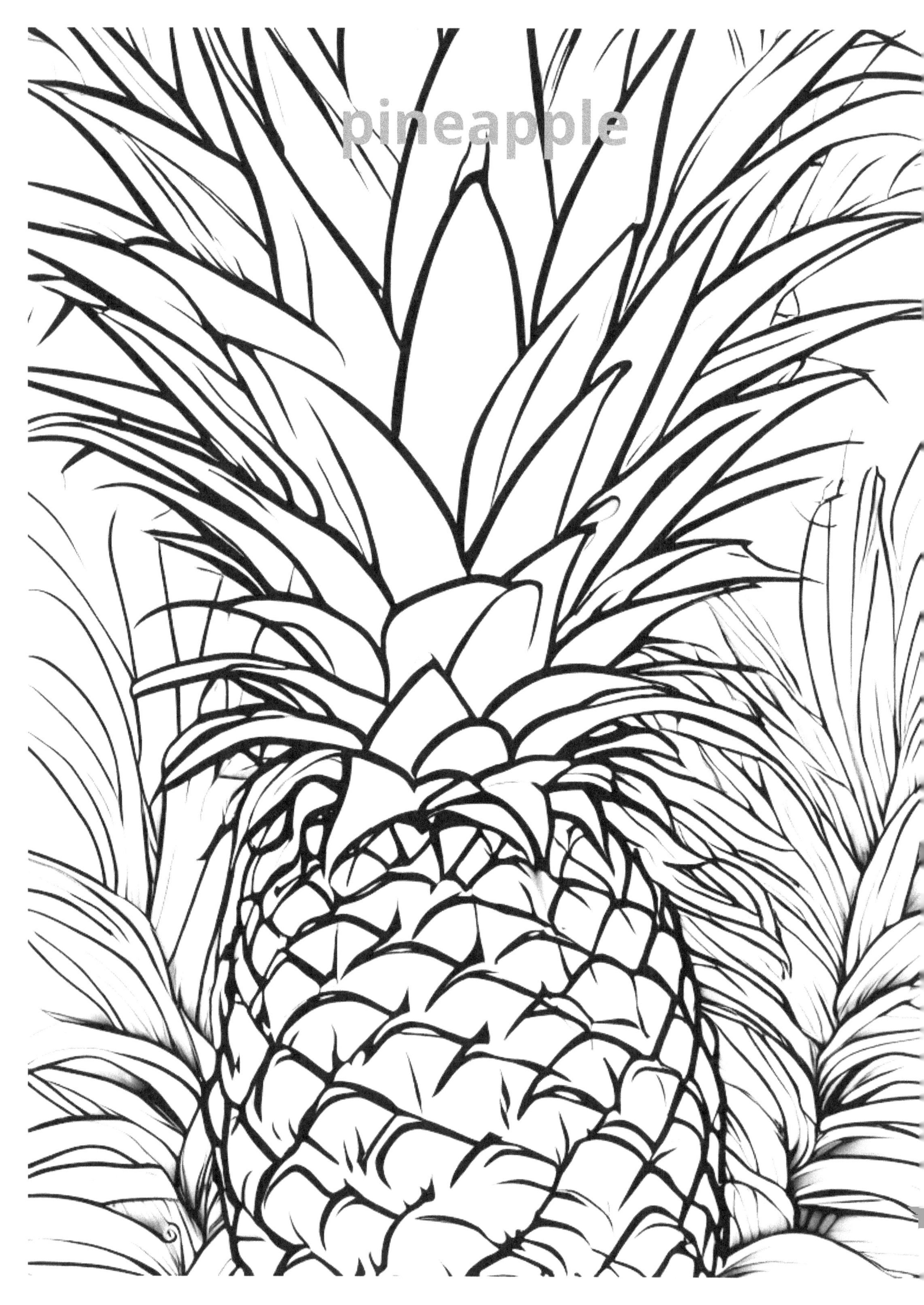

pineapple

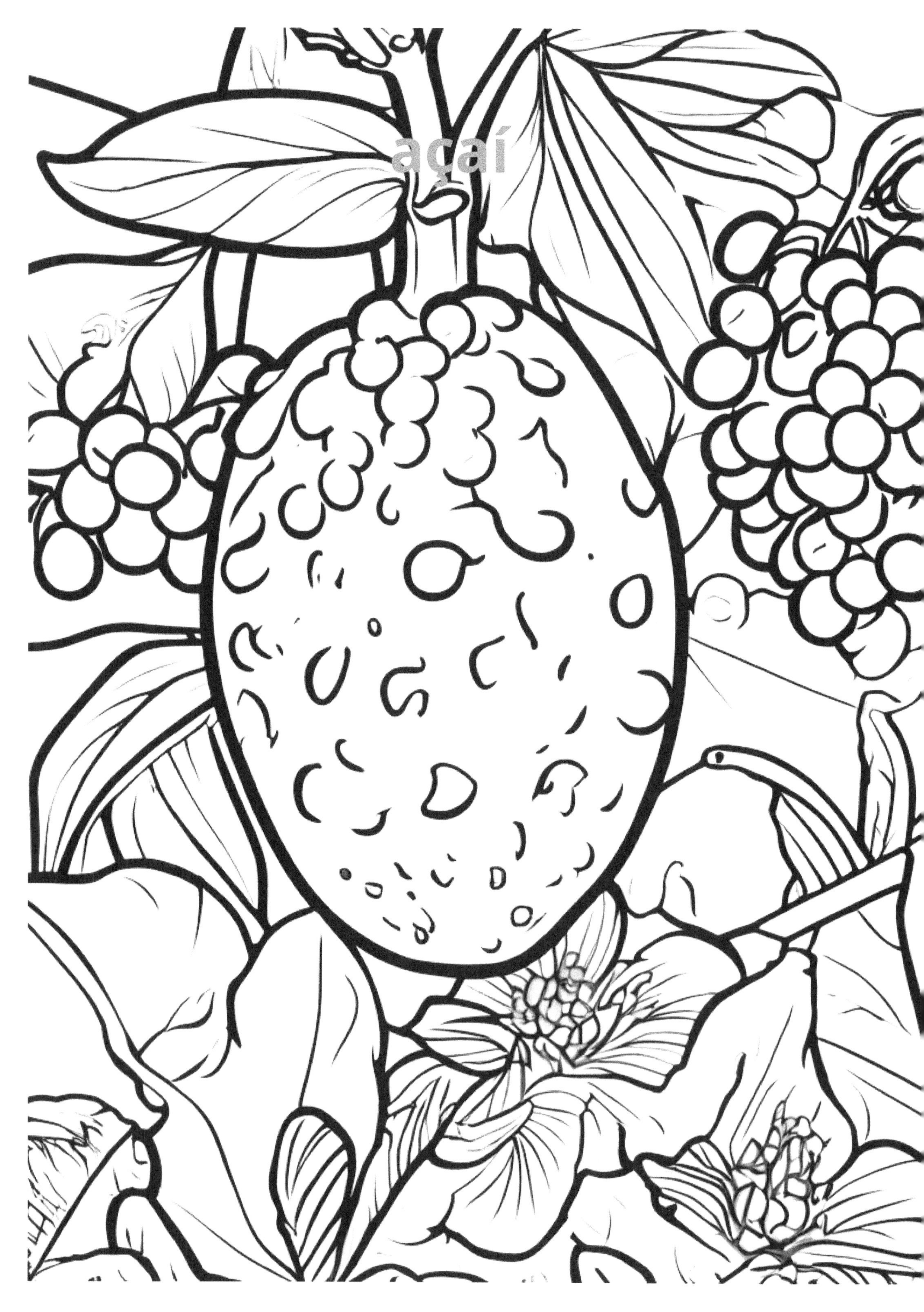

açaí

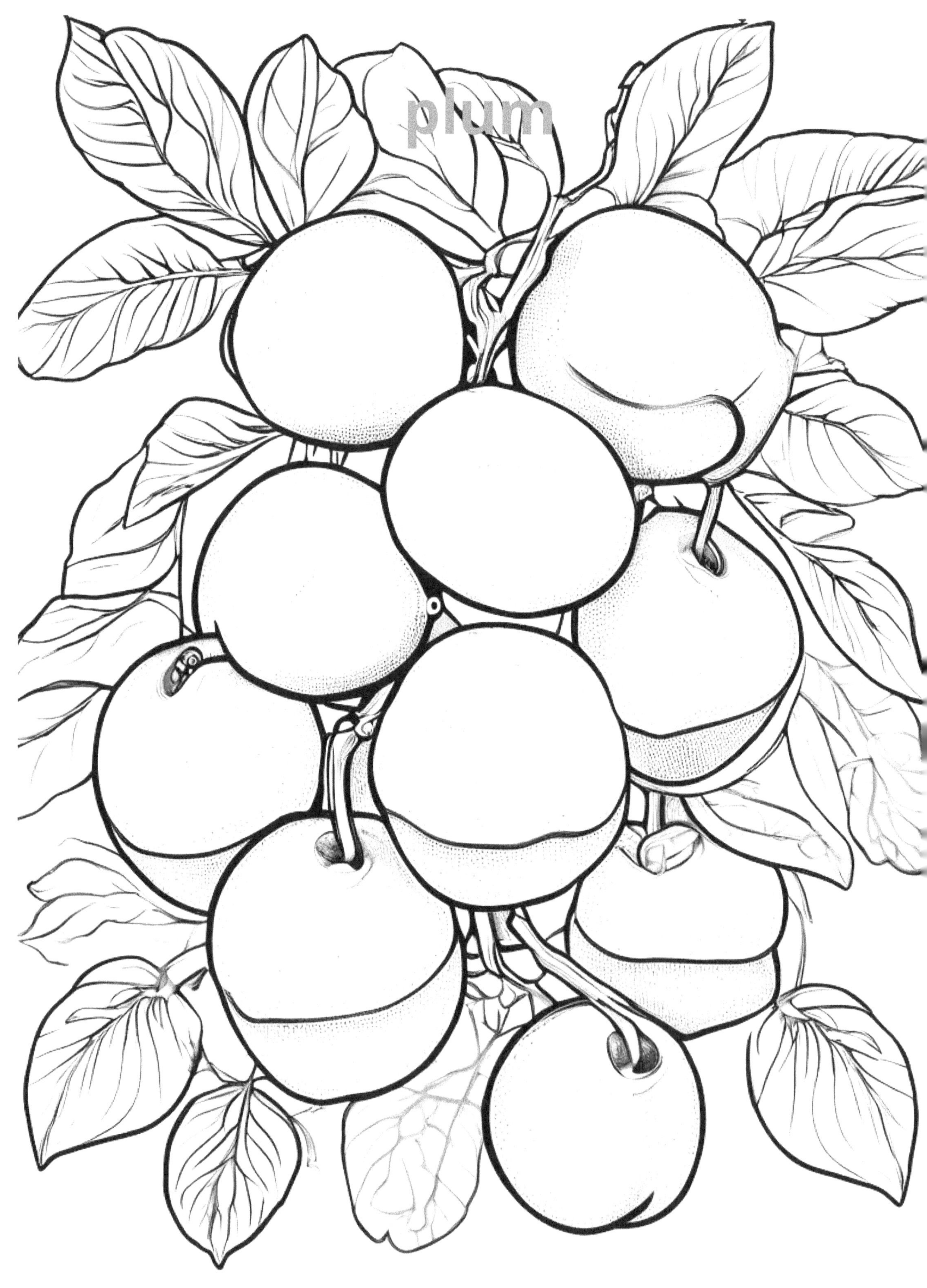
plum

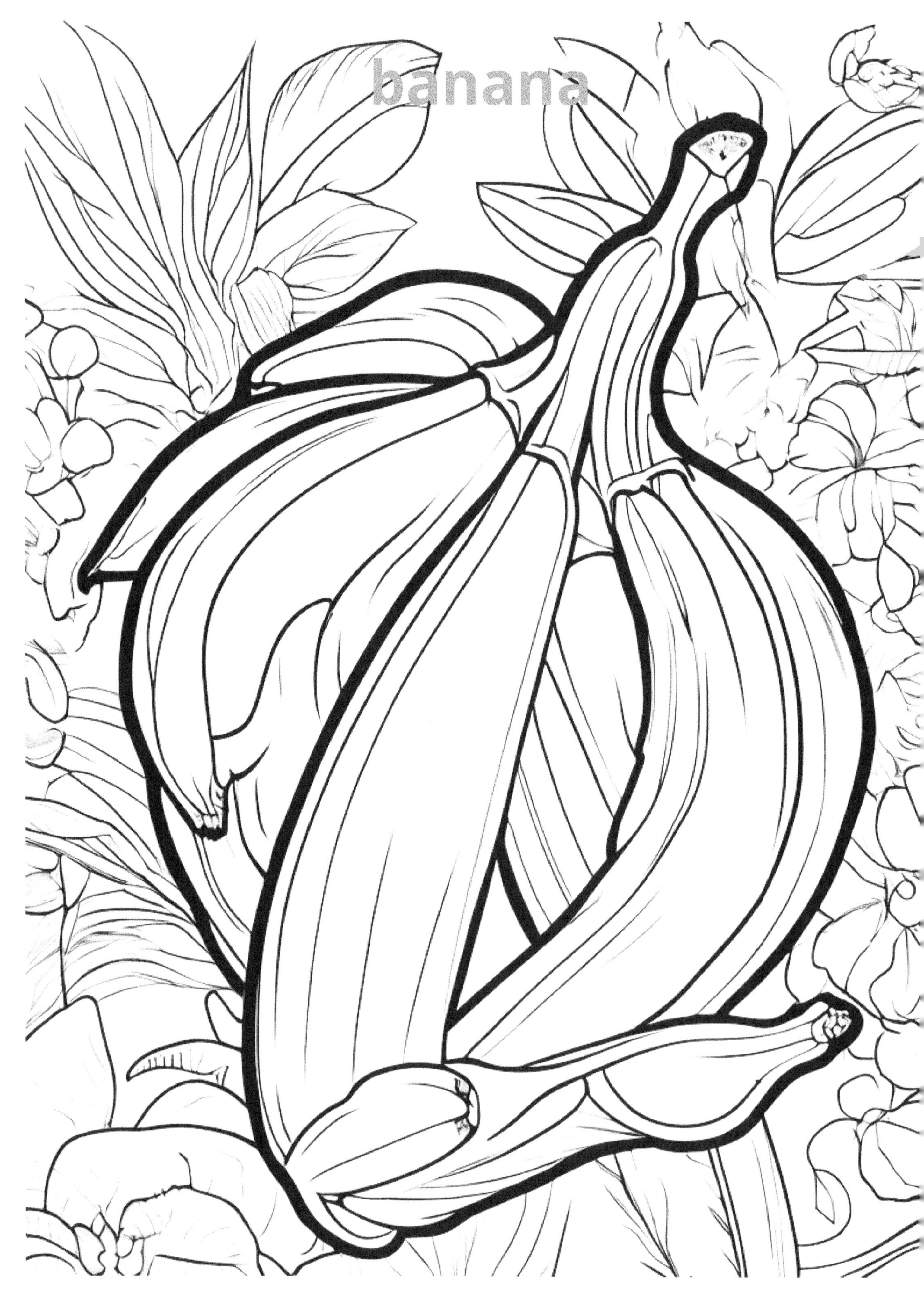
banana

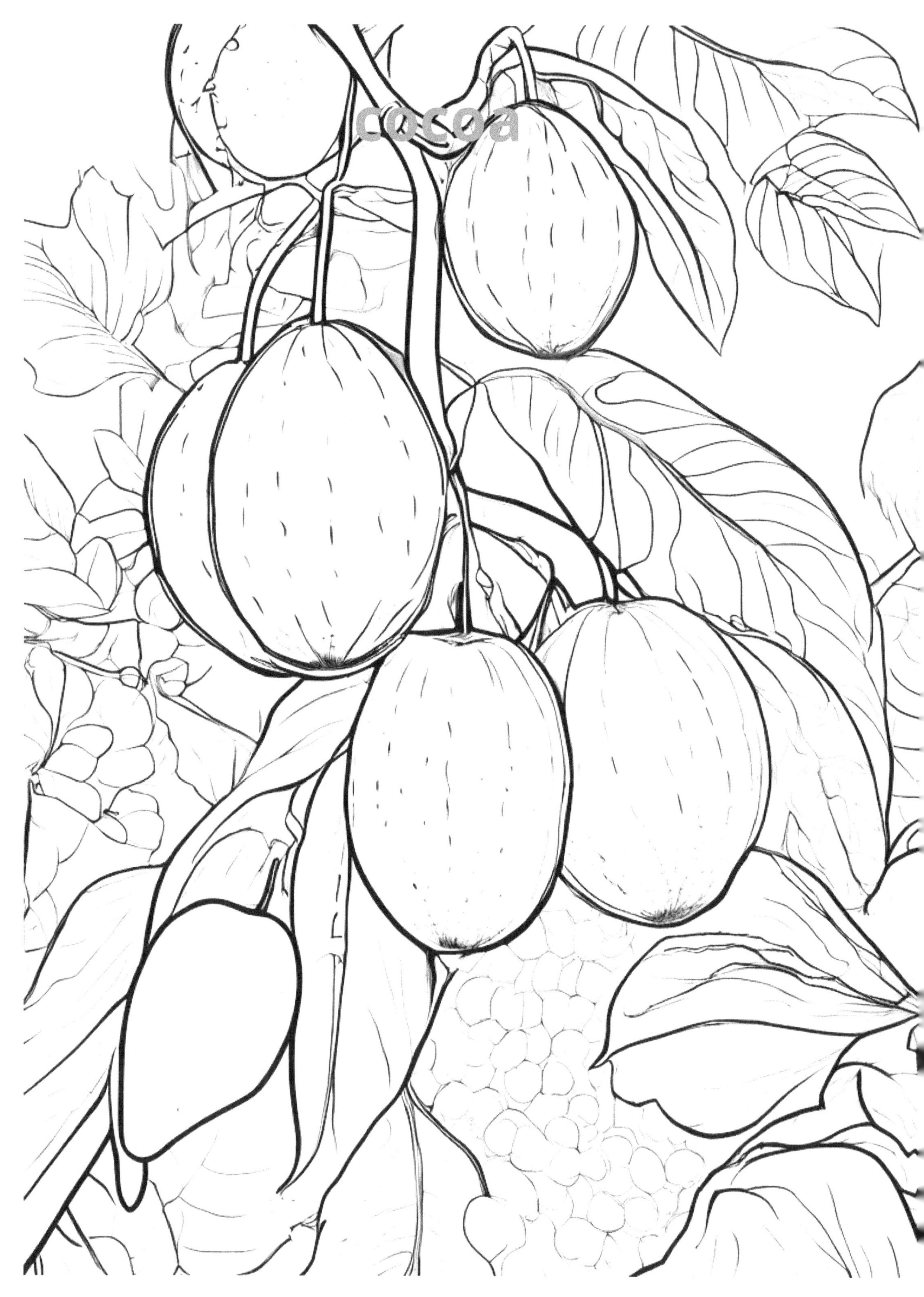
cocoa

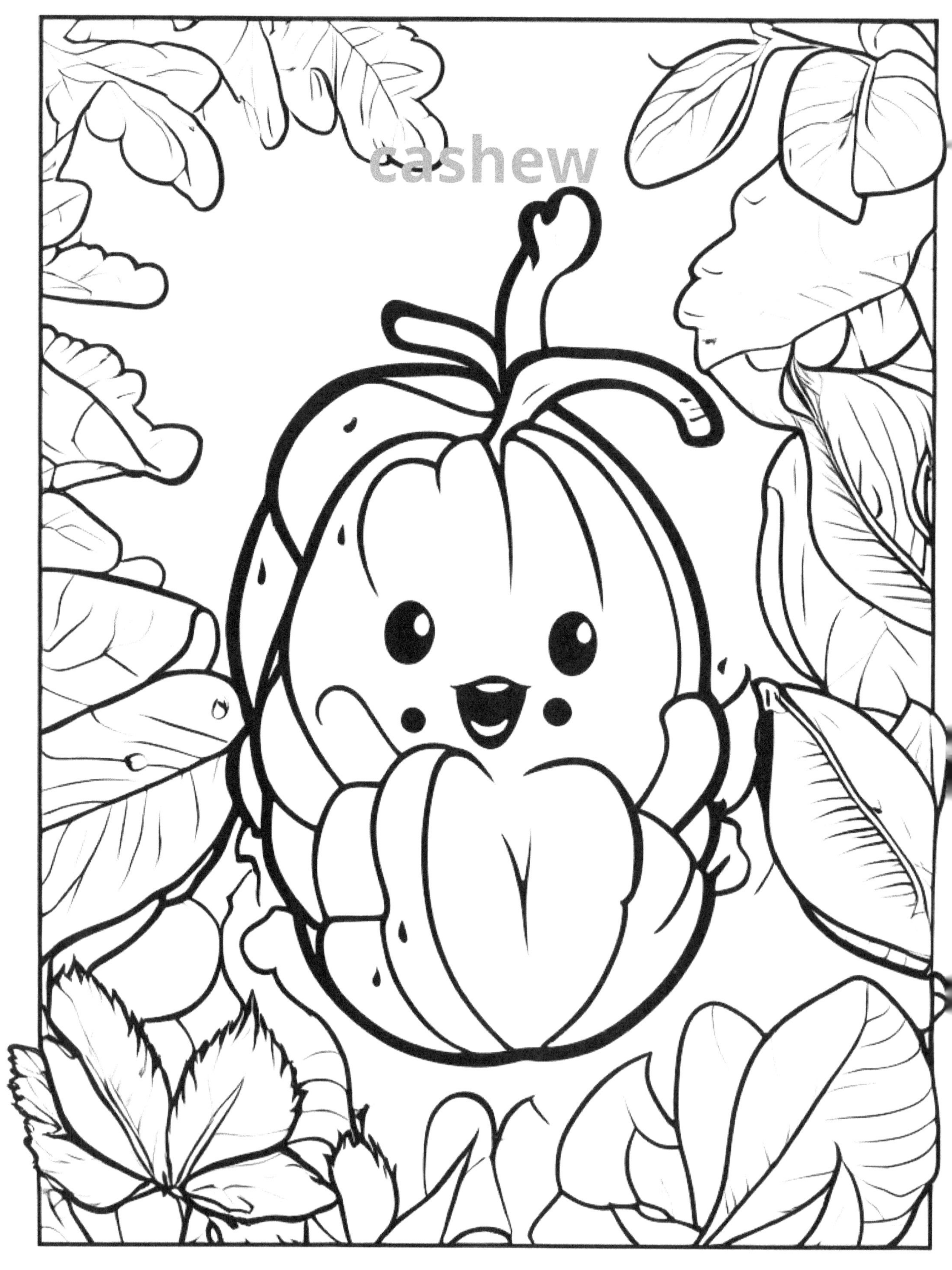
cashew

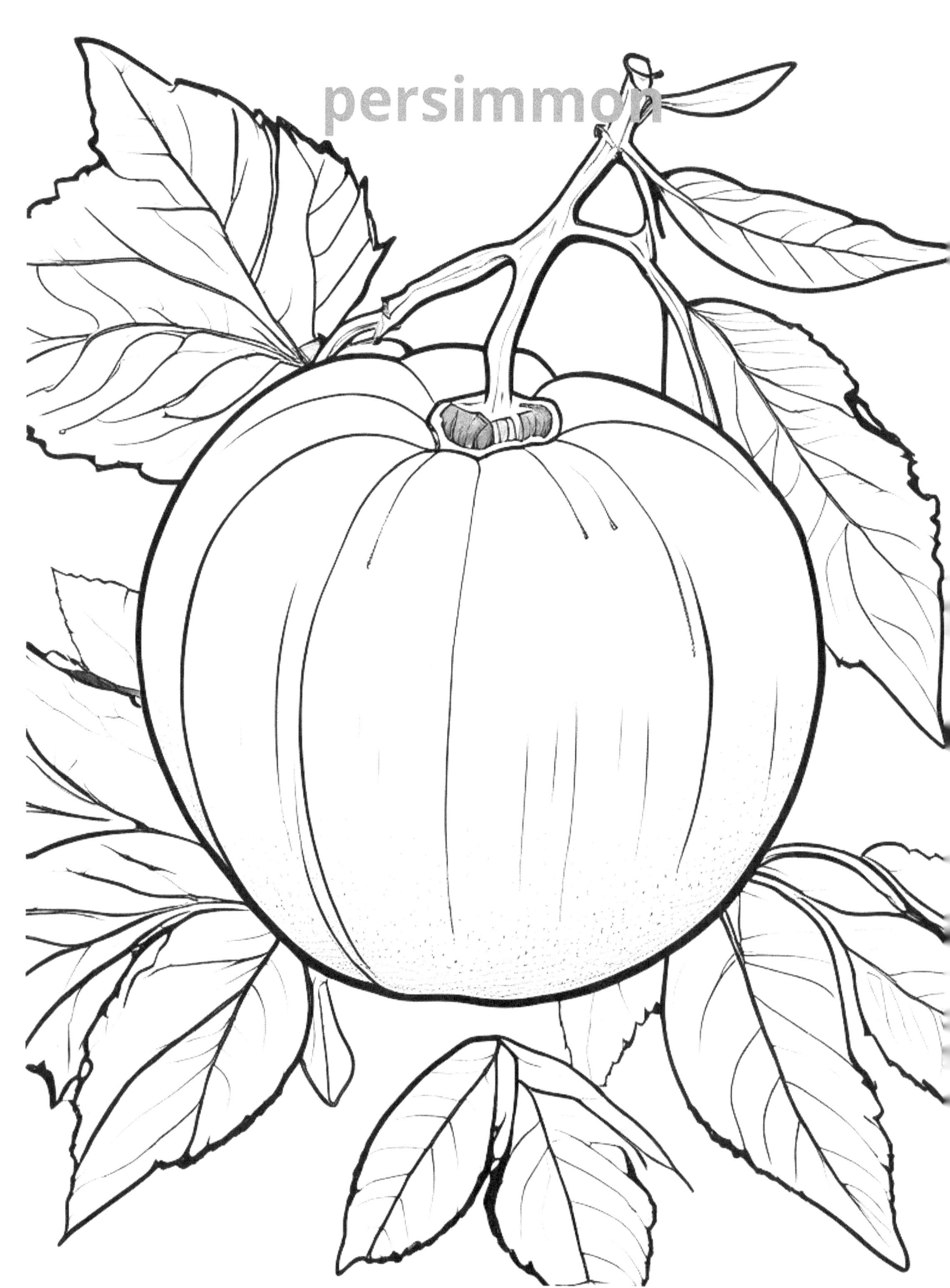
persimmon

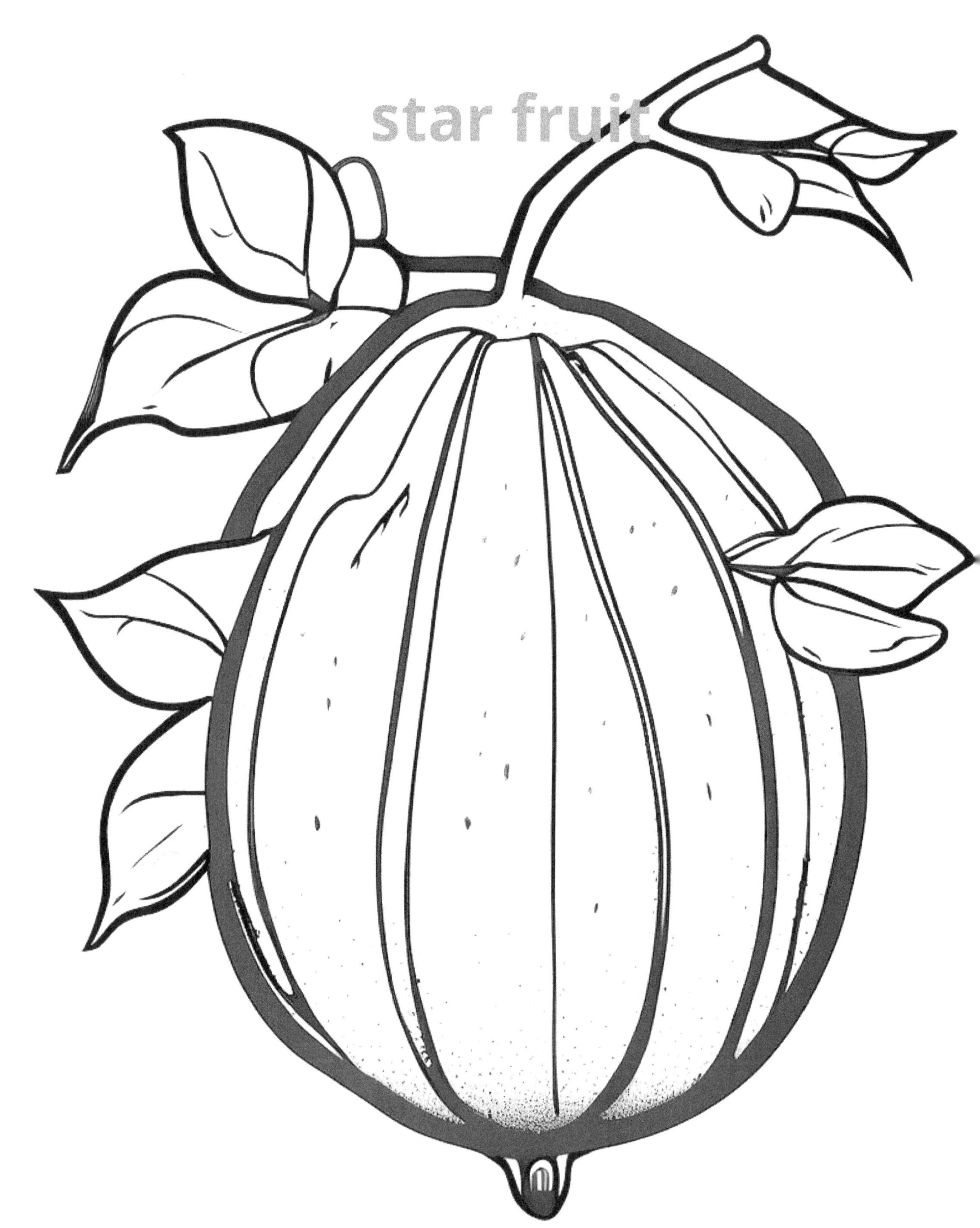

star fruit

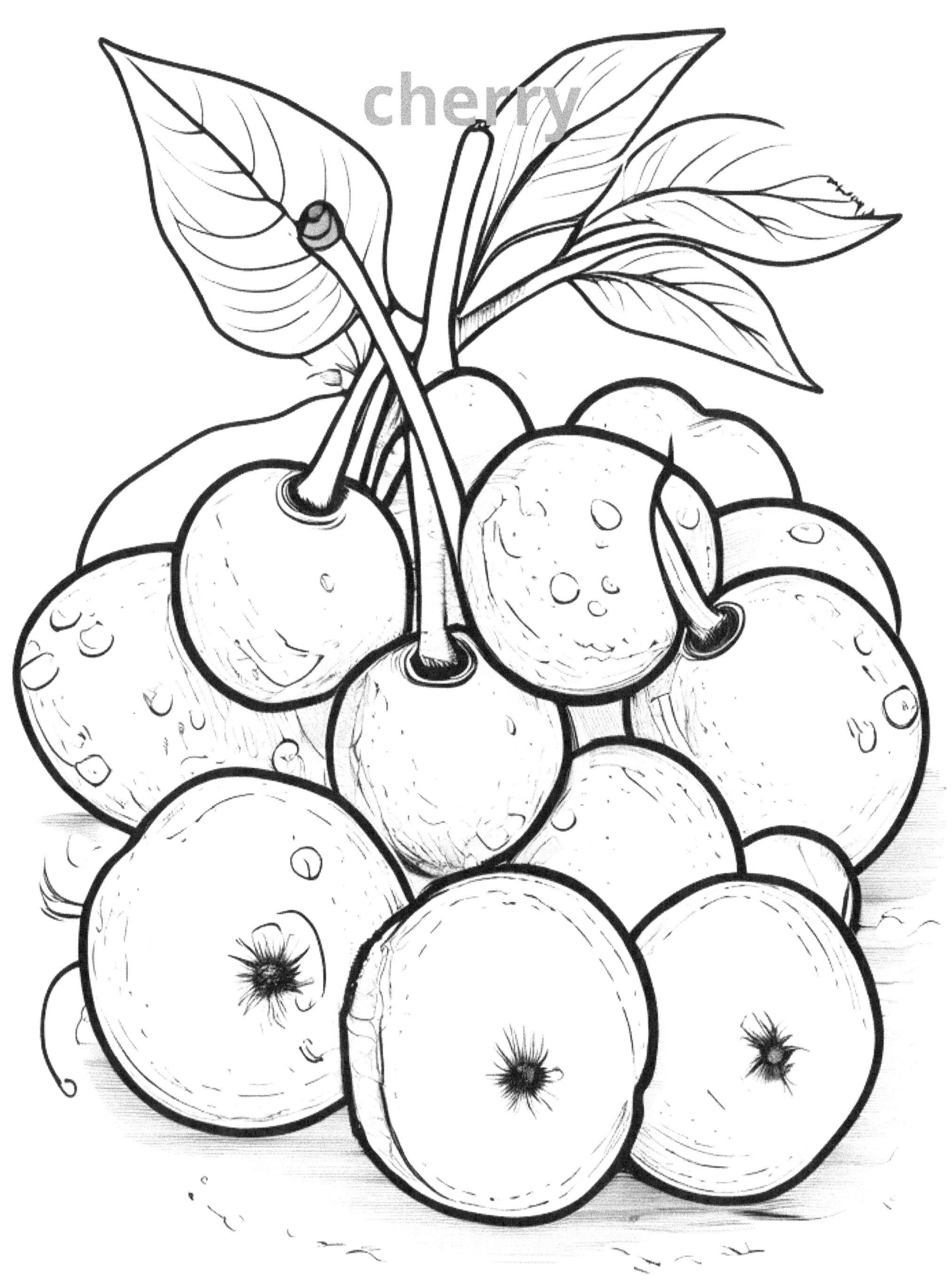

cherry

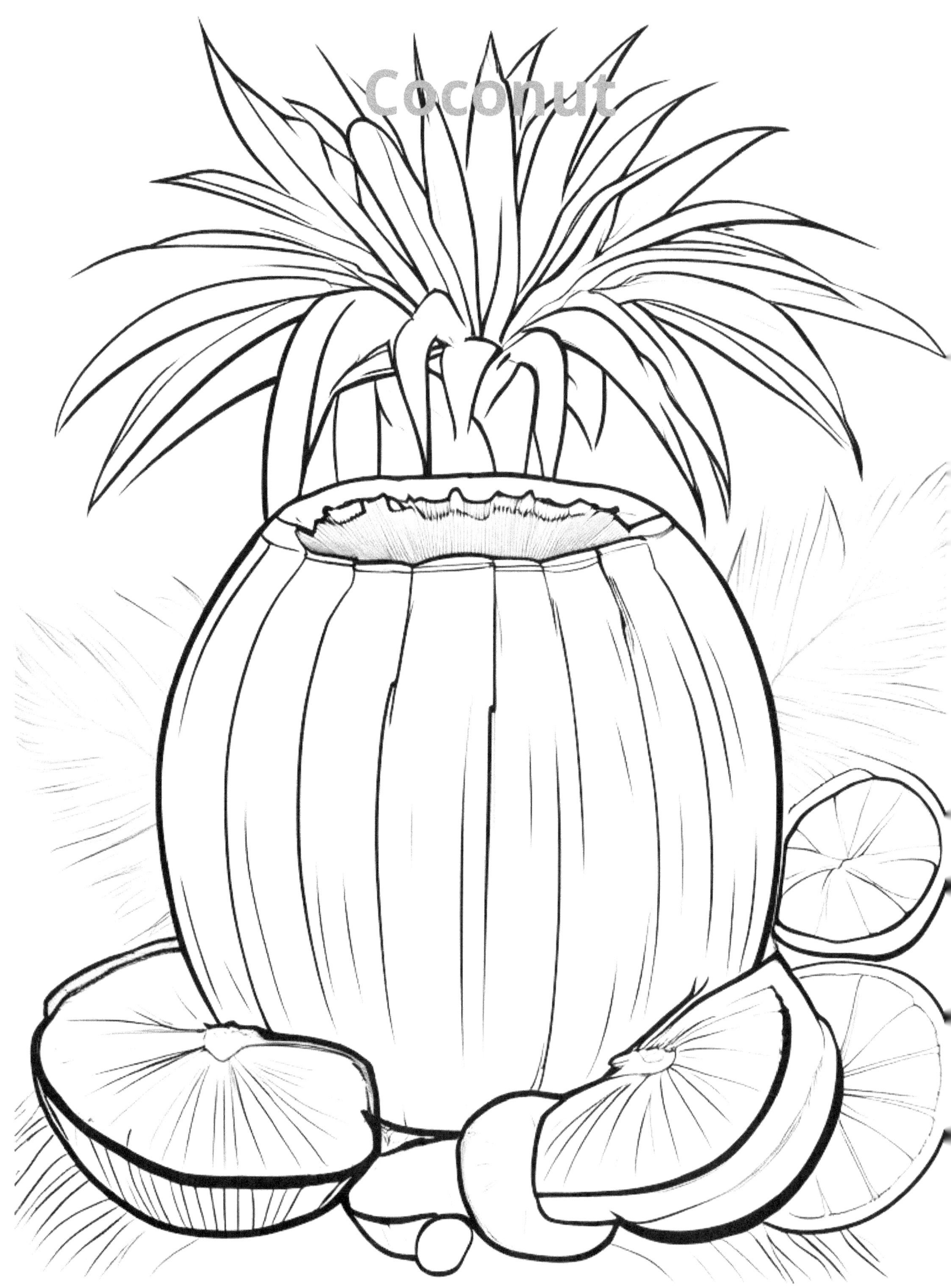
Coconut

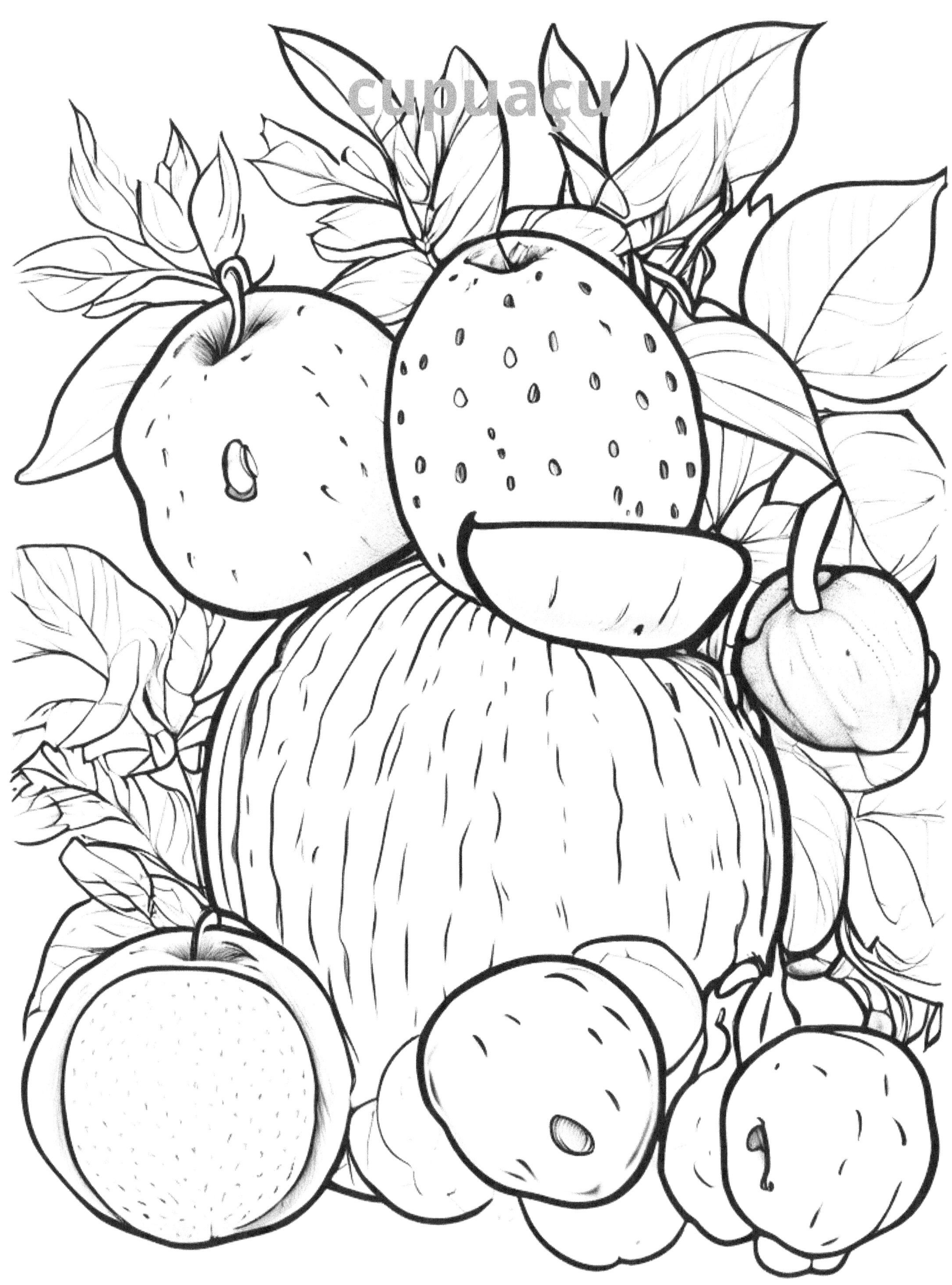
cupuaçu

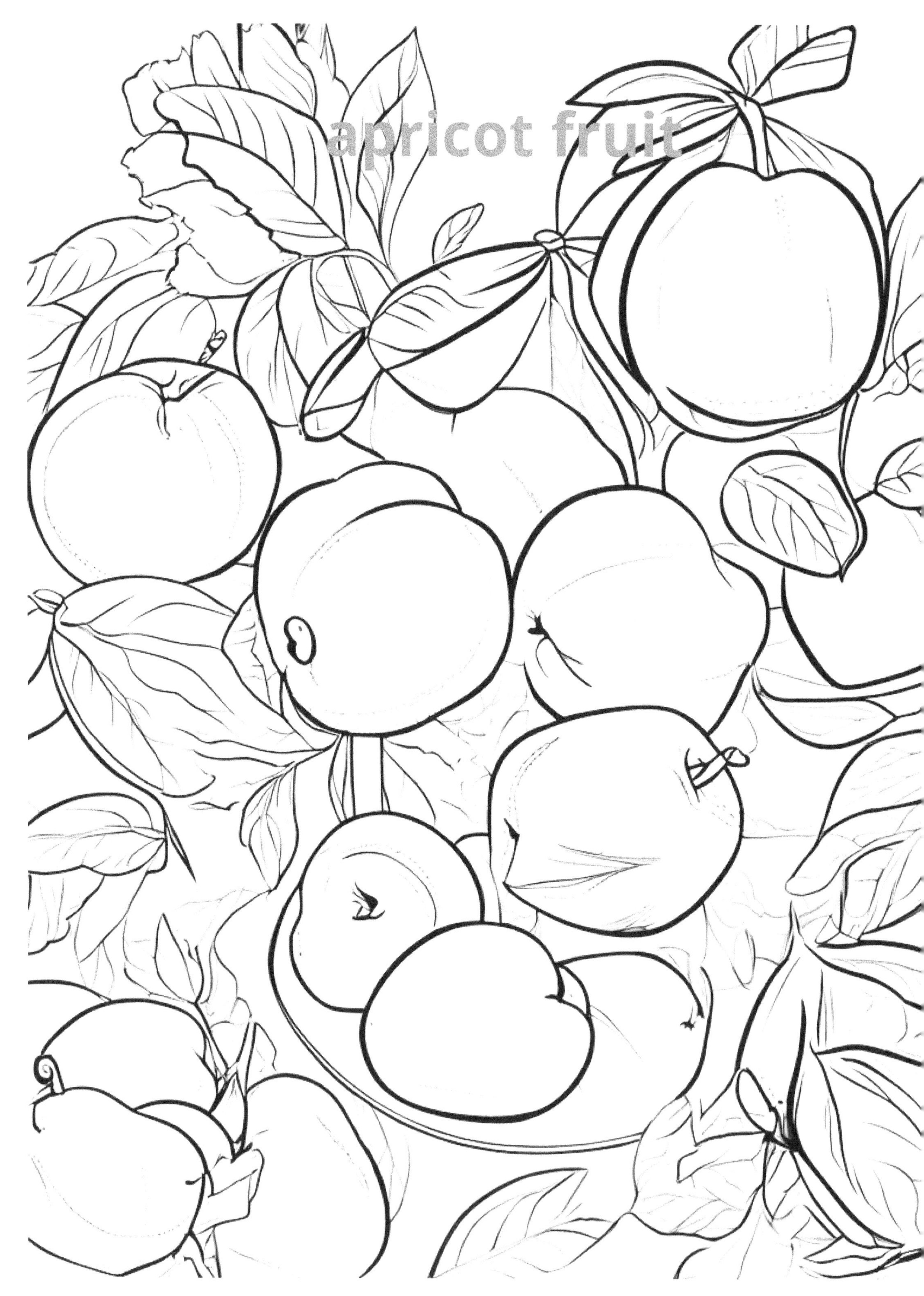

apricot fruit

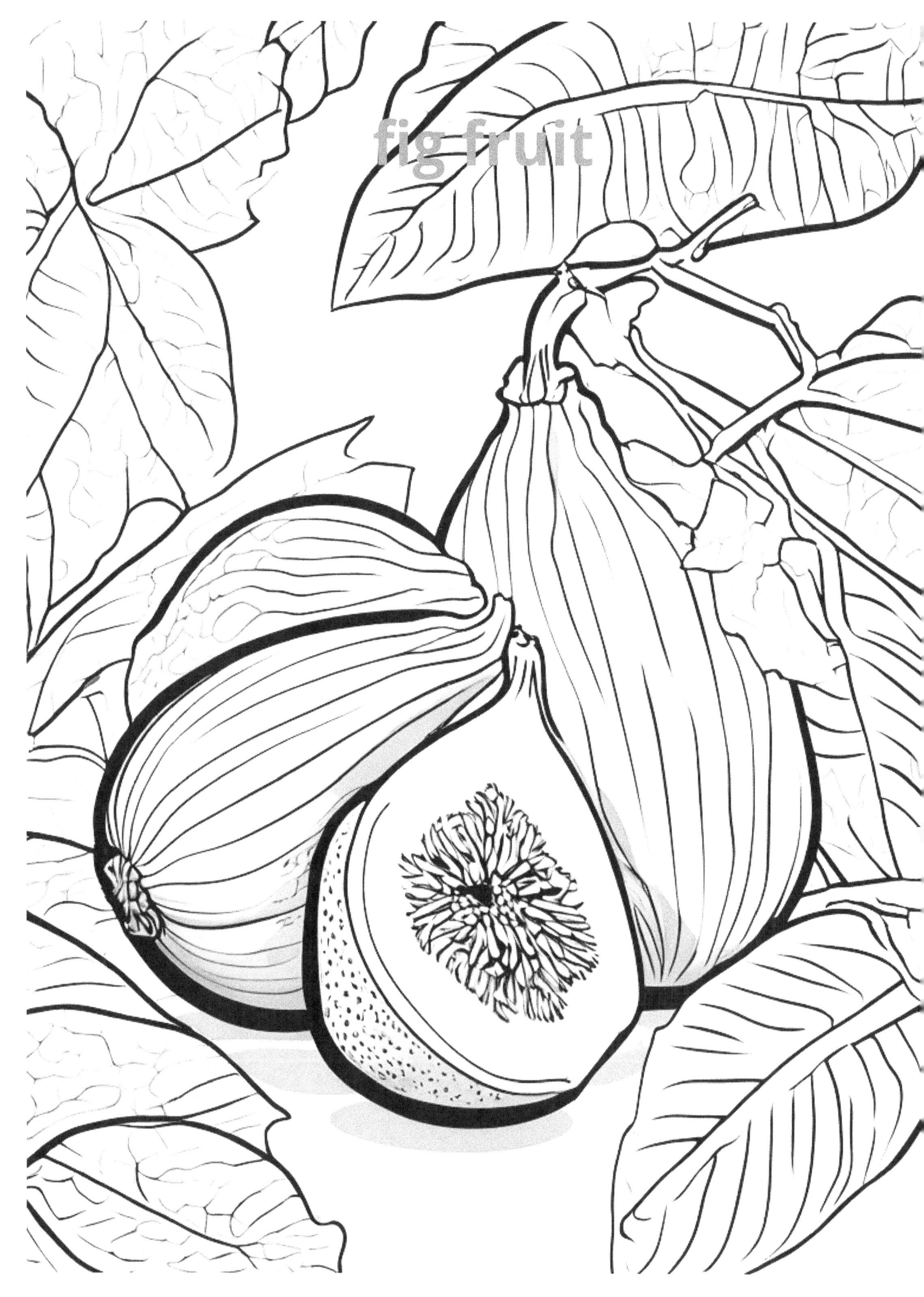
fig fruit

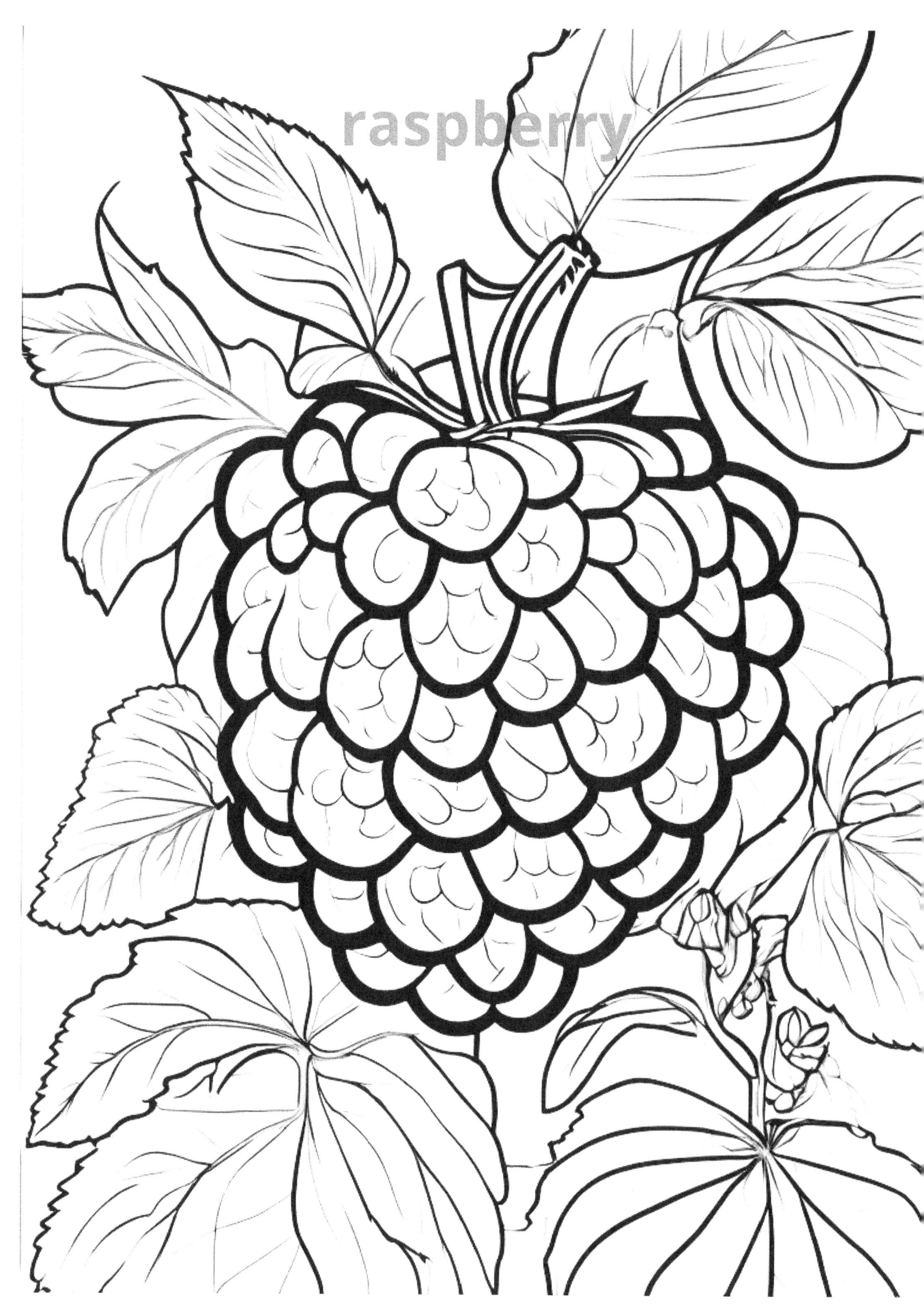
raspberry

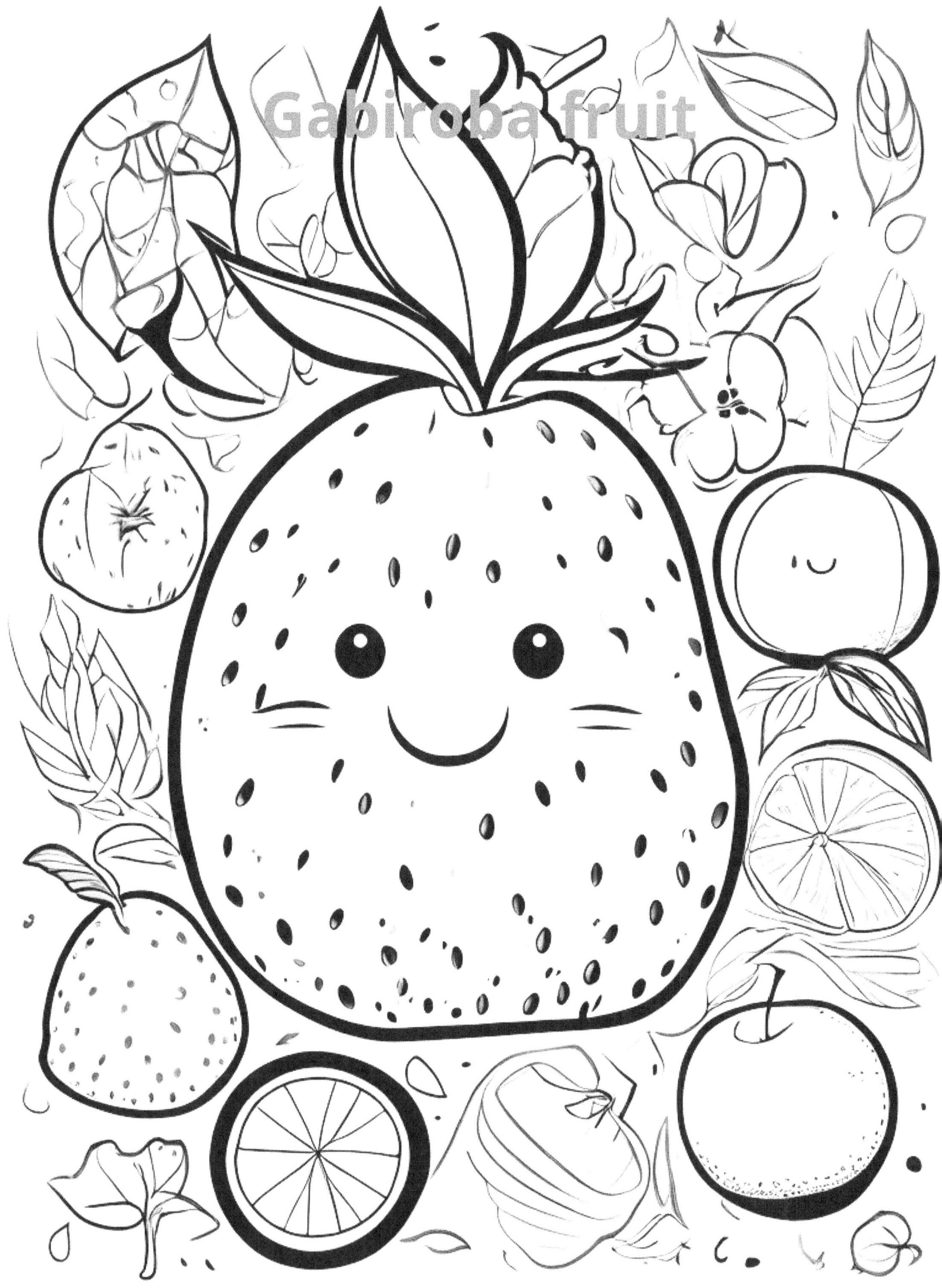
Gabiroba fruit

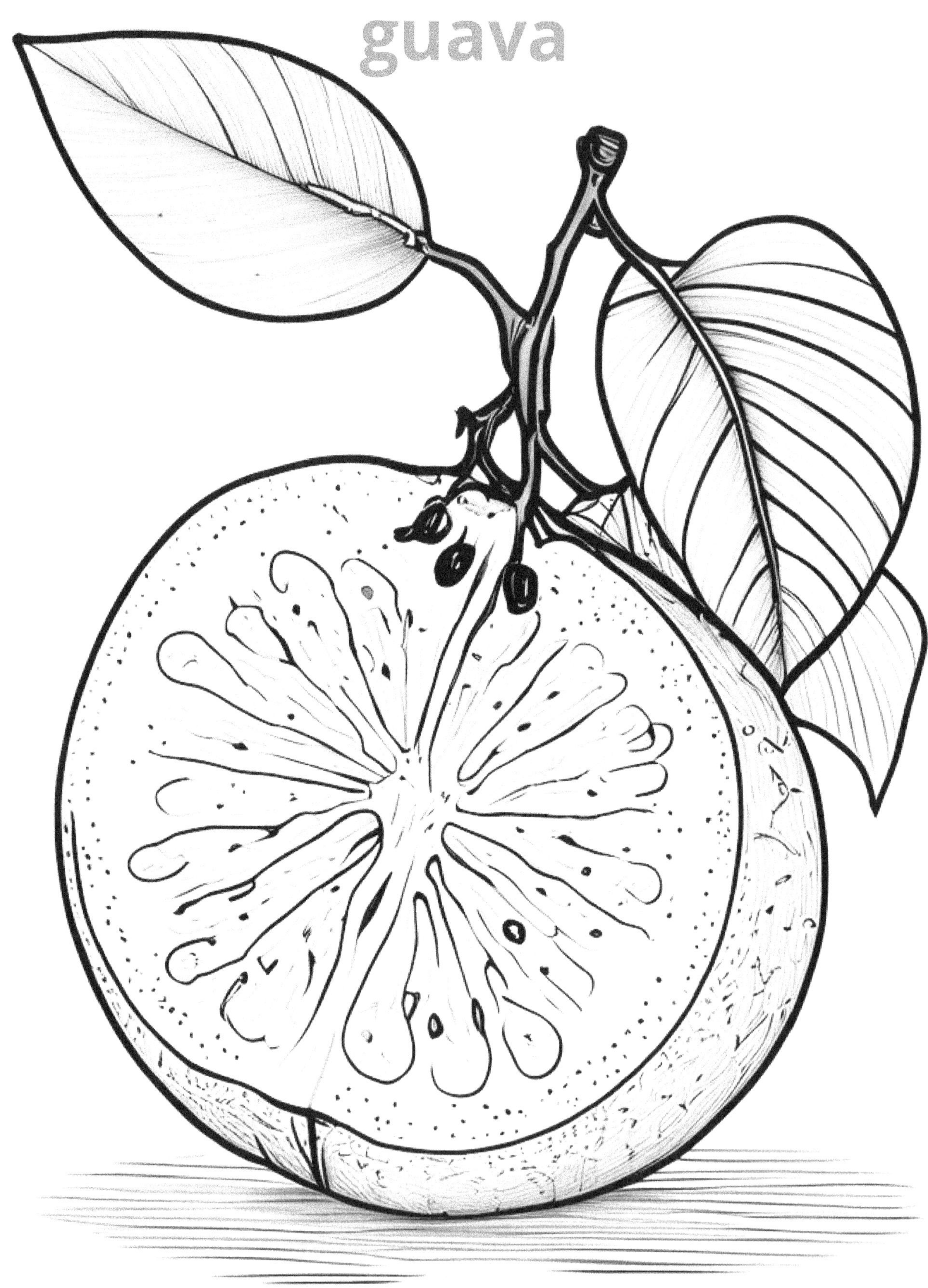

guava

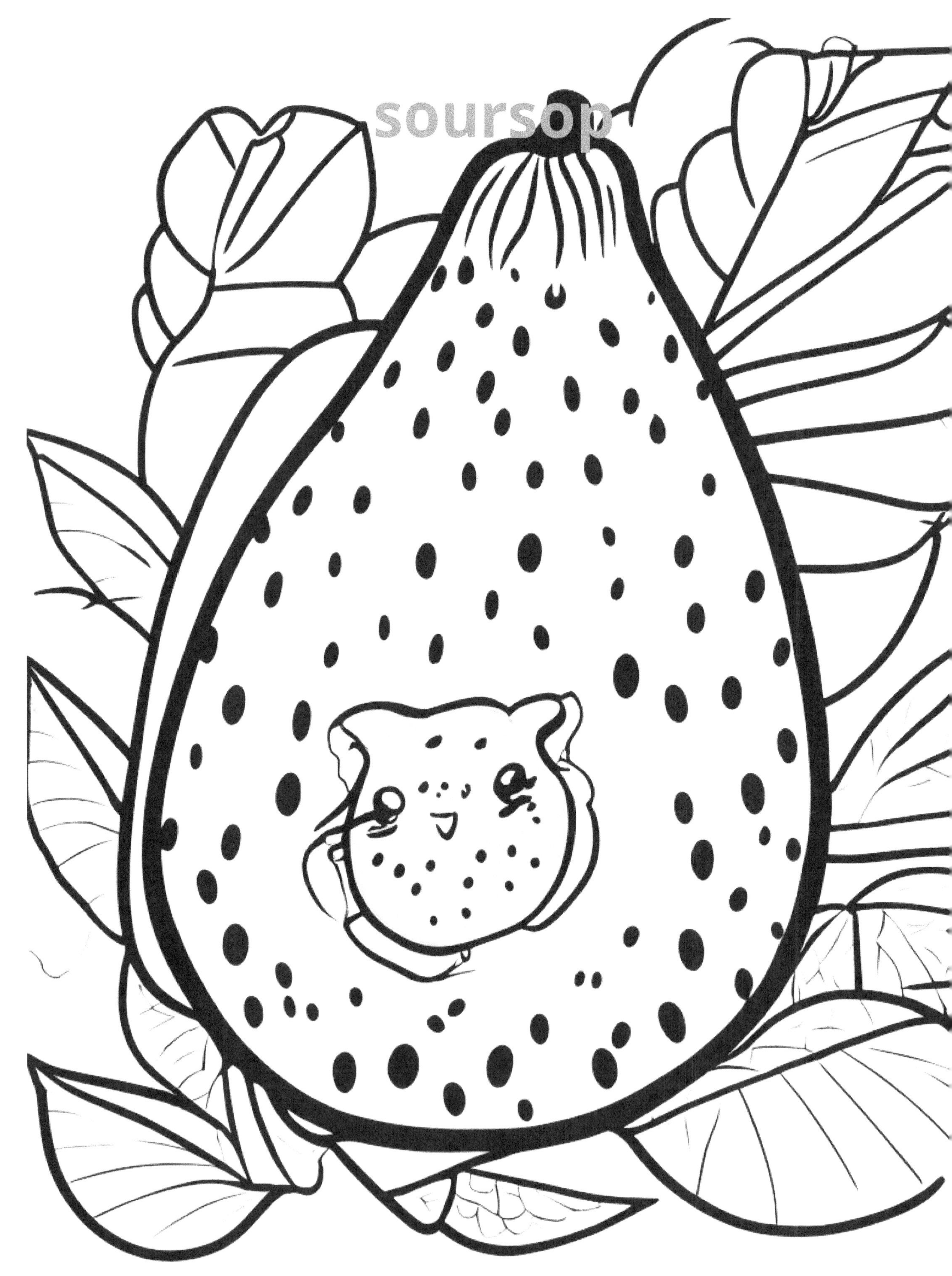

soursop

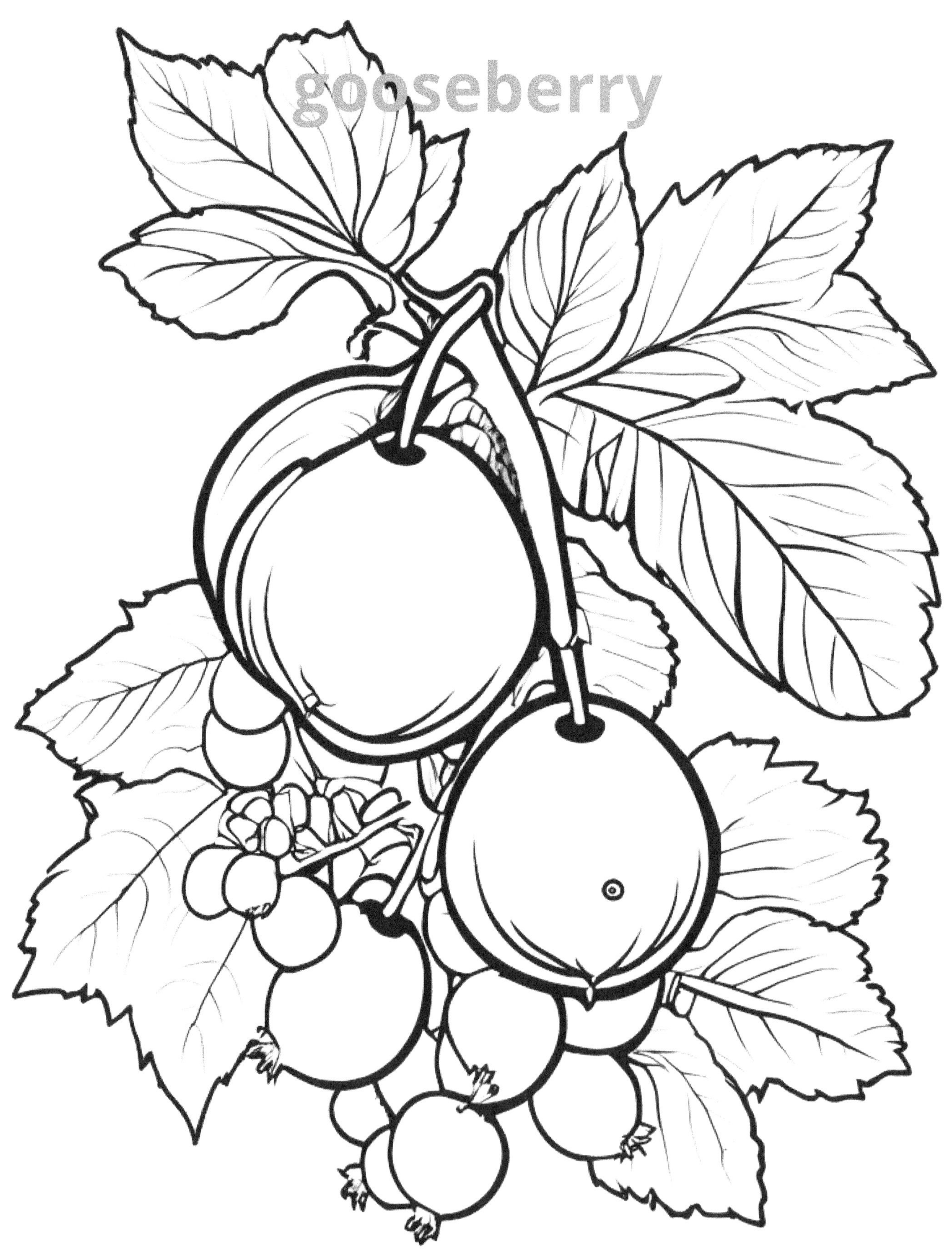

gooseberry

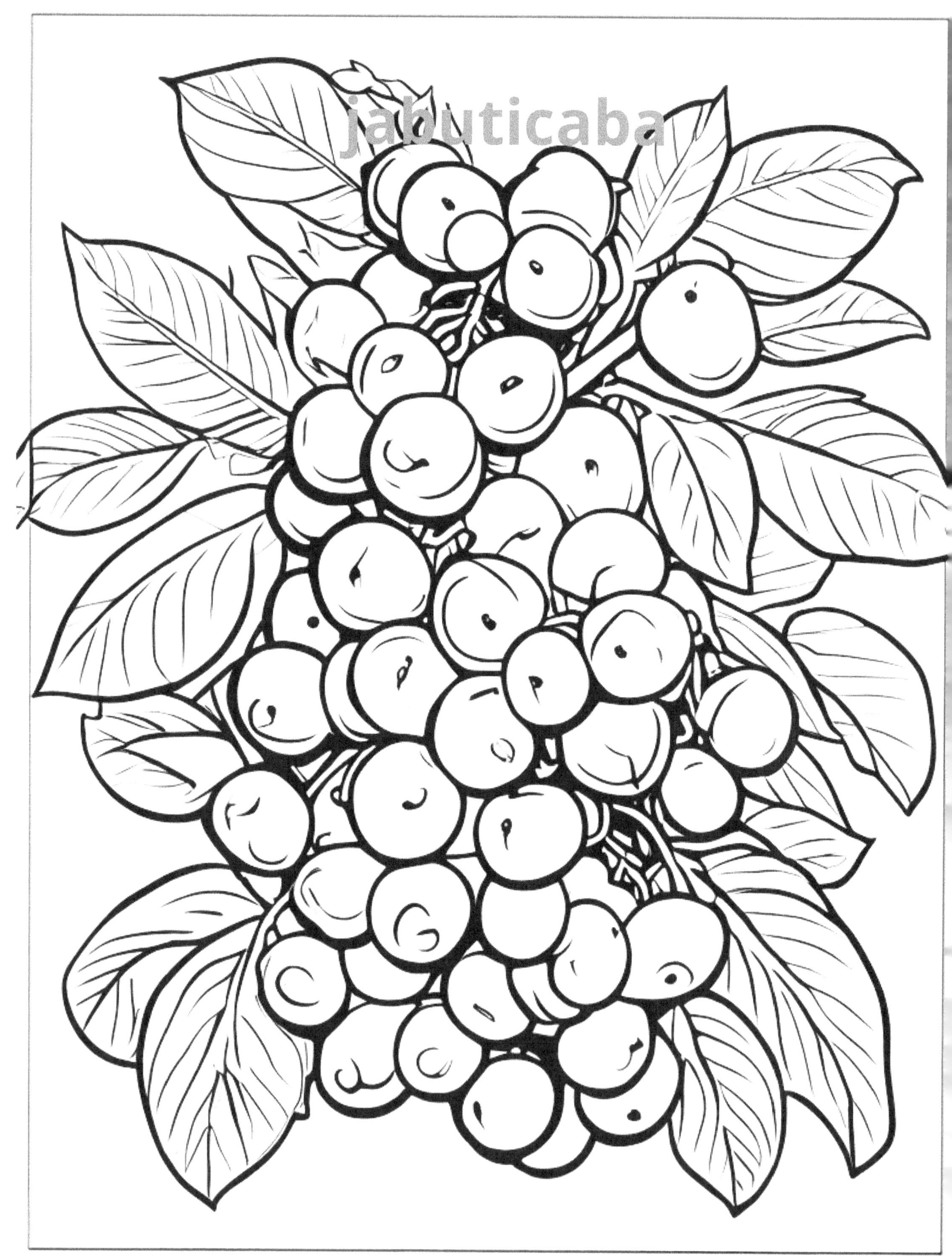
jabuticaba

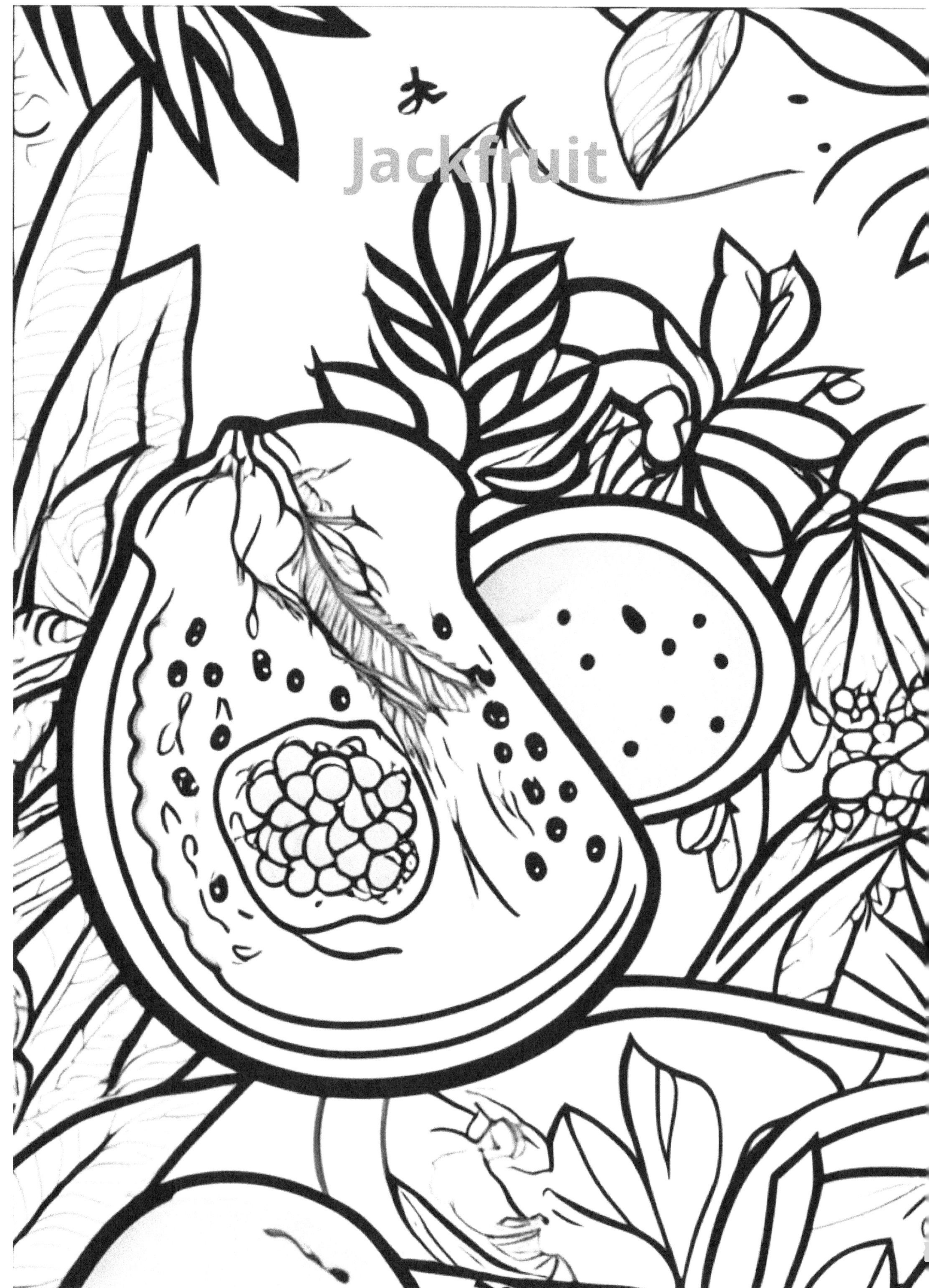
Jackfruit

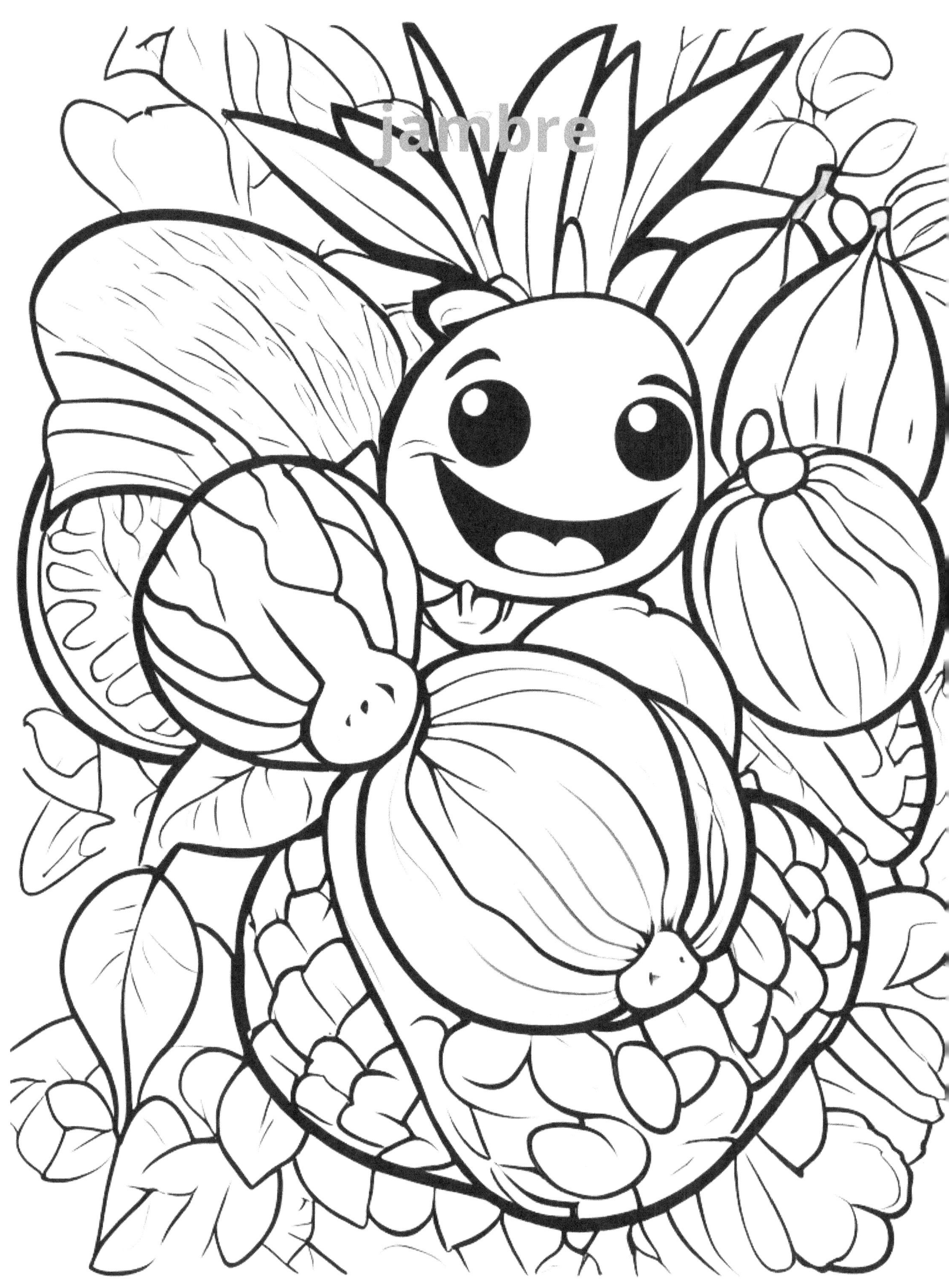
jambre

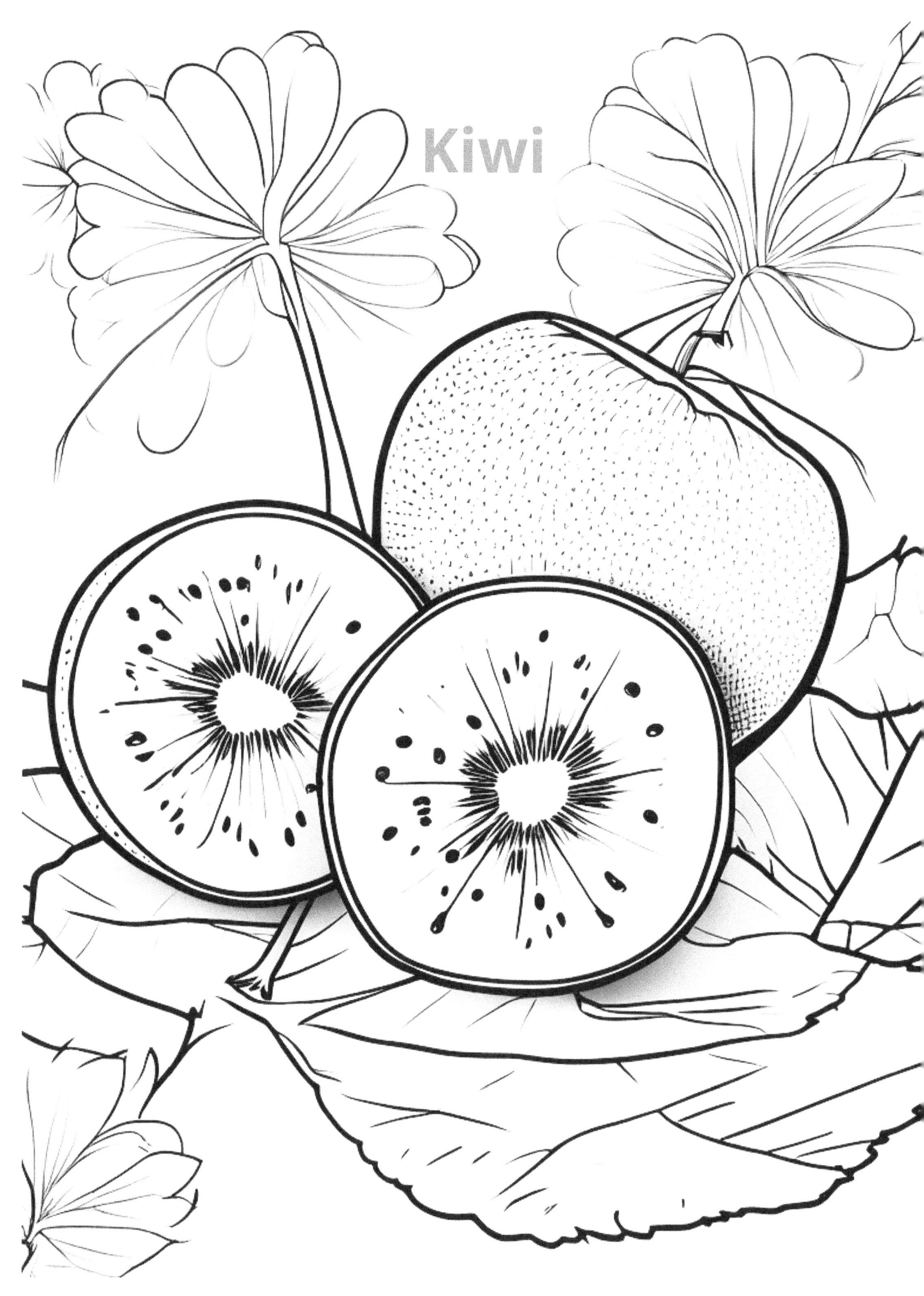

Kiwi

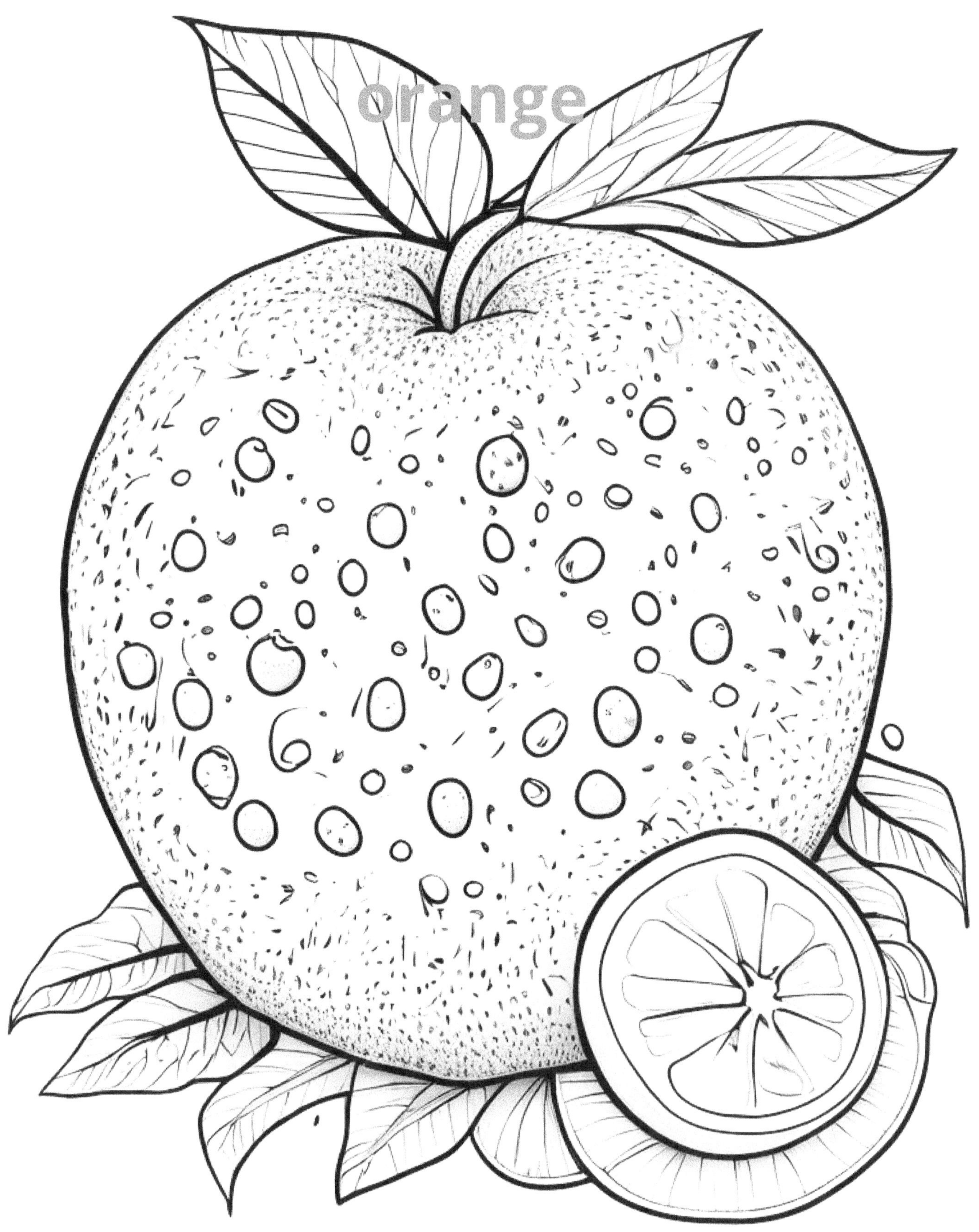
orange

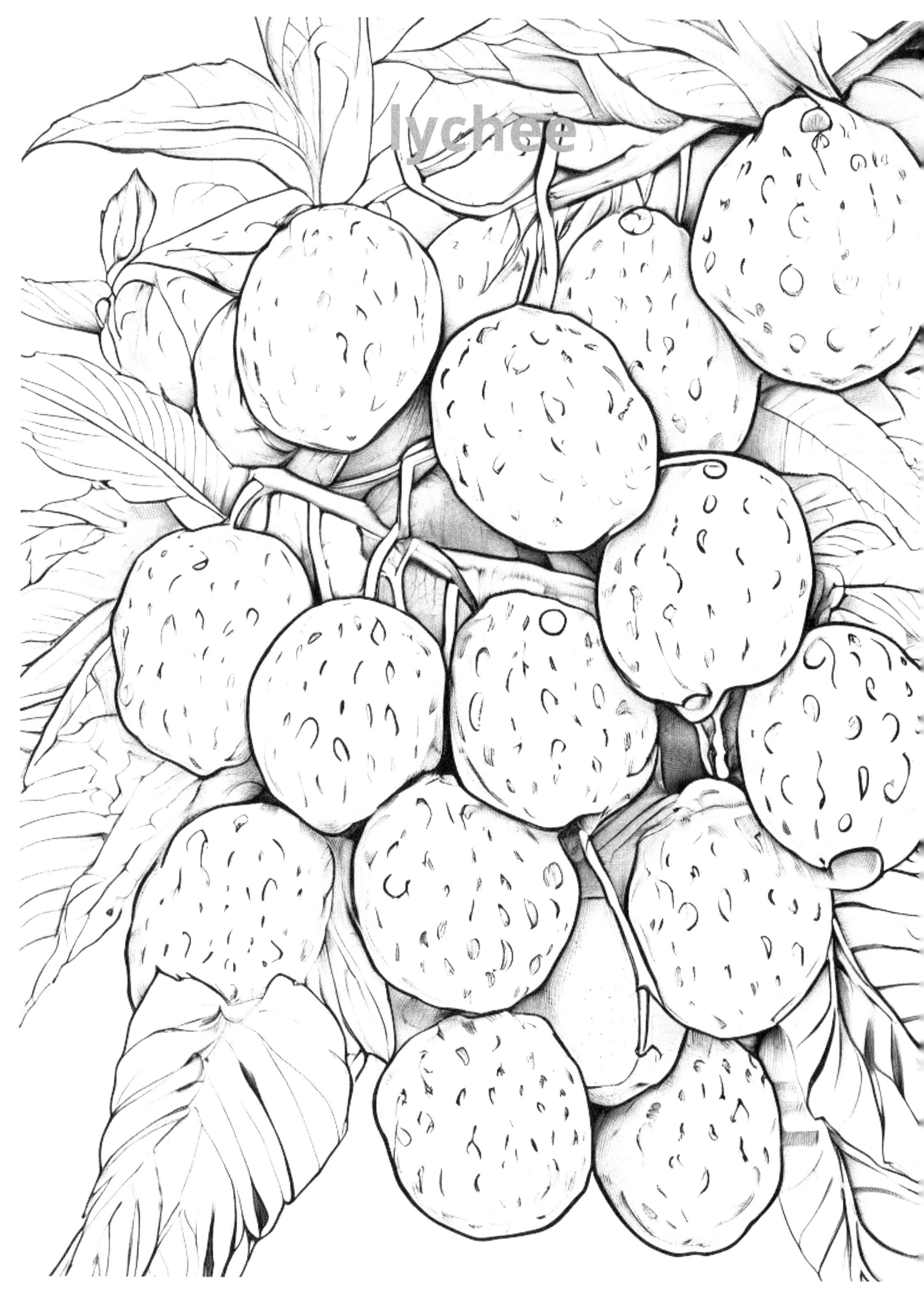
lychee

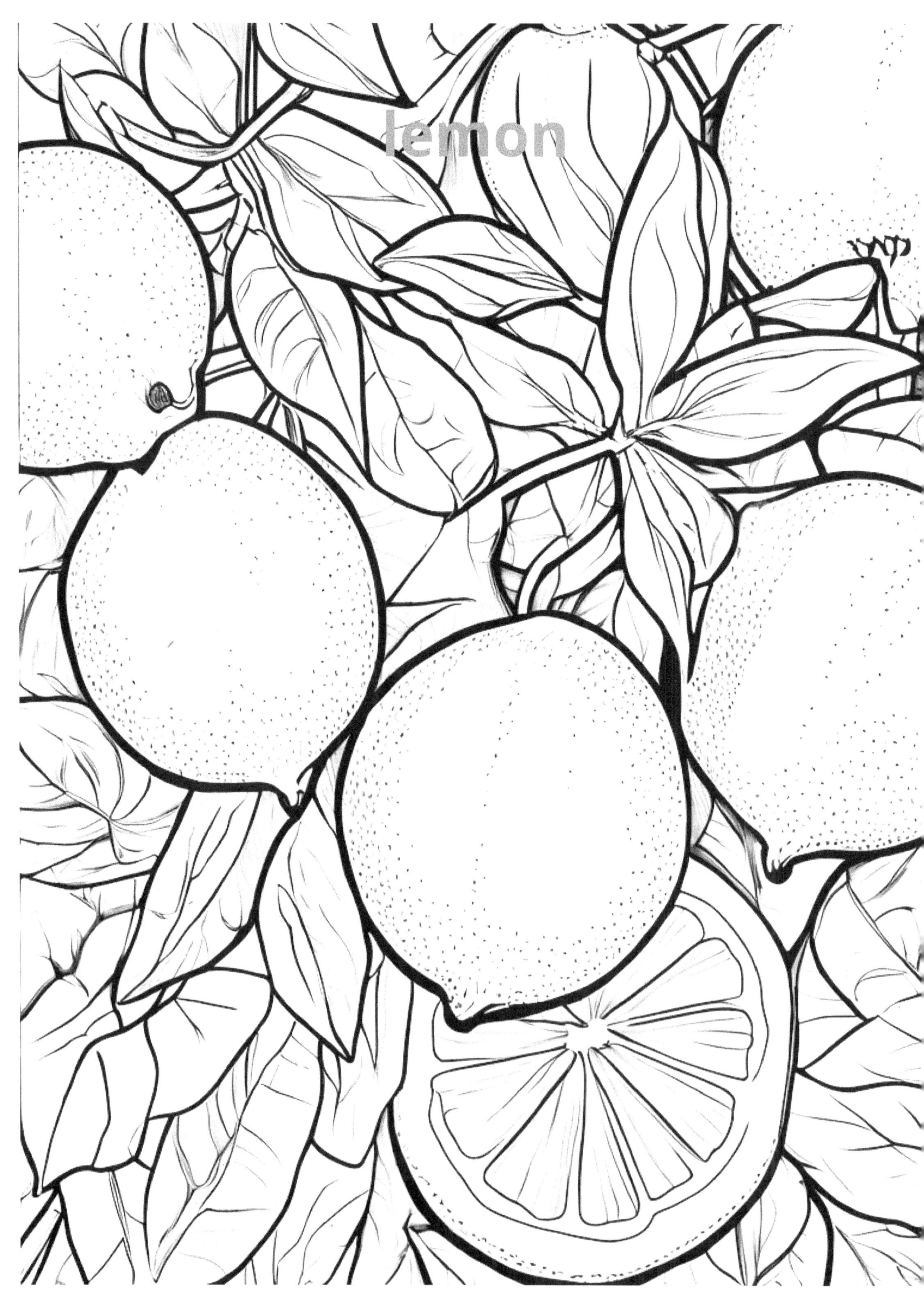

lemon

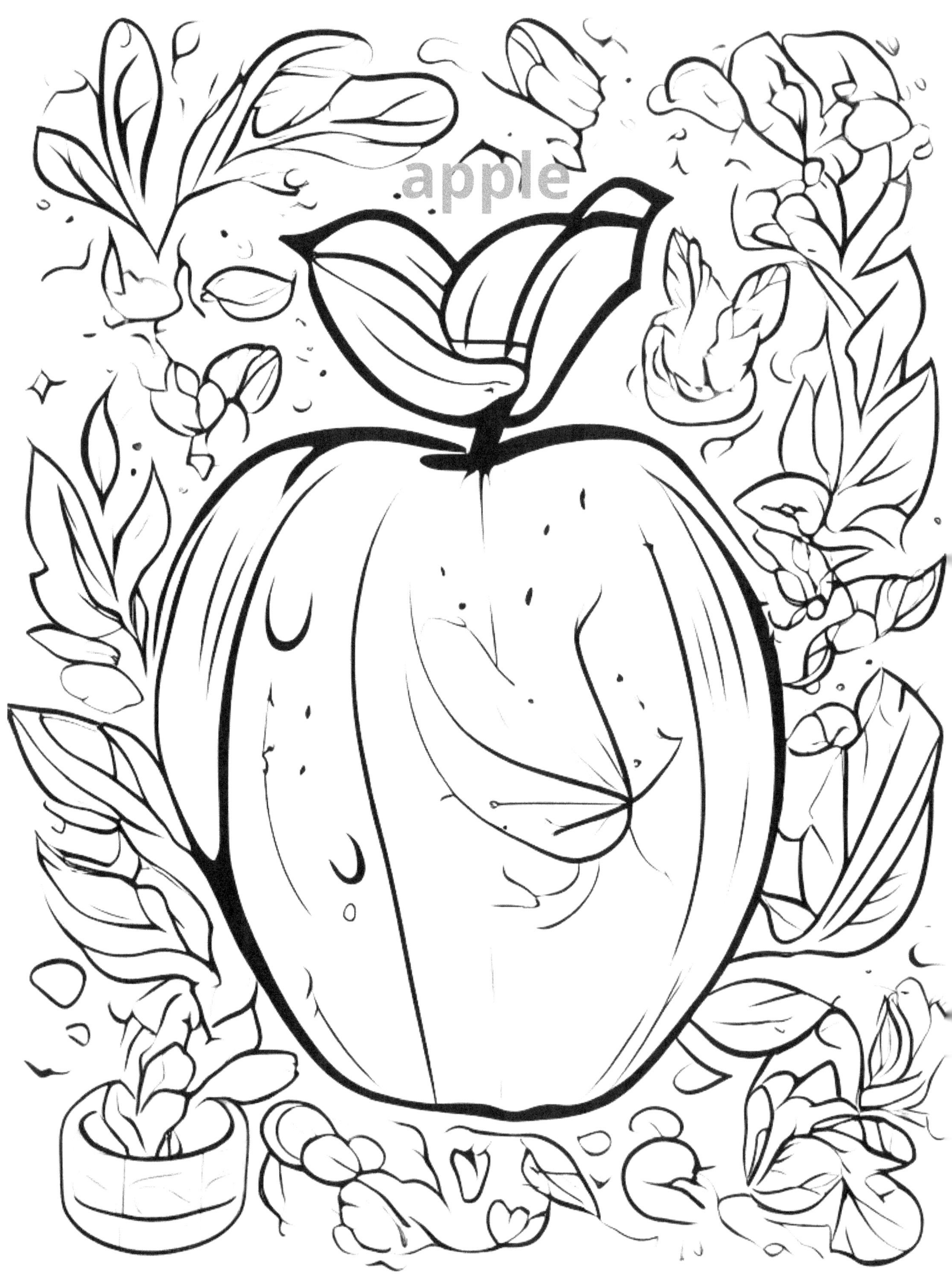
apple

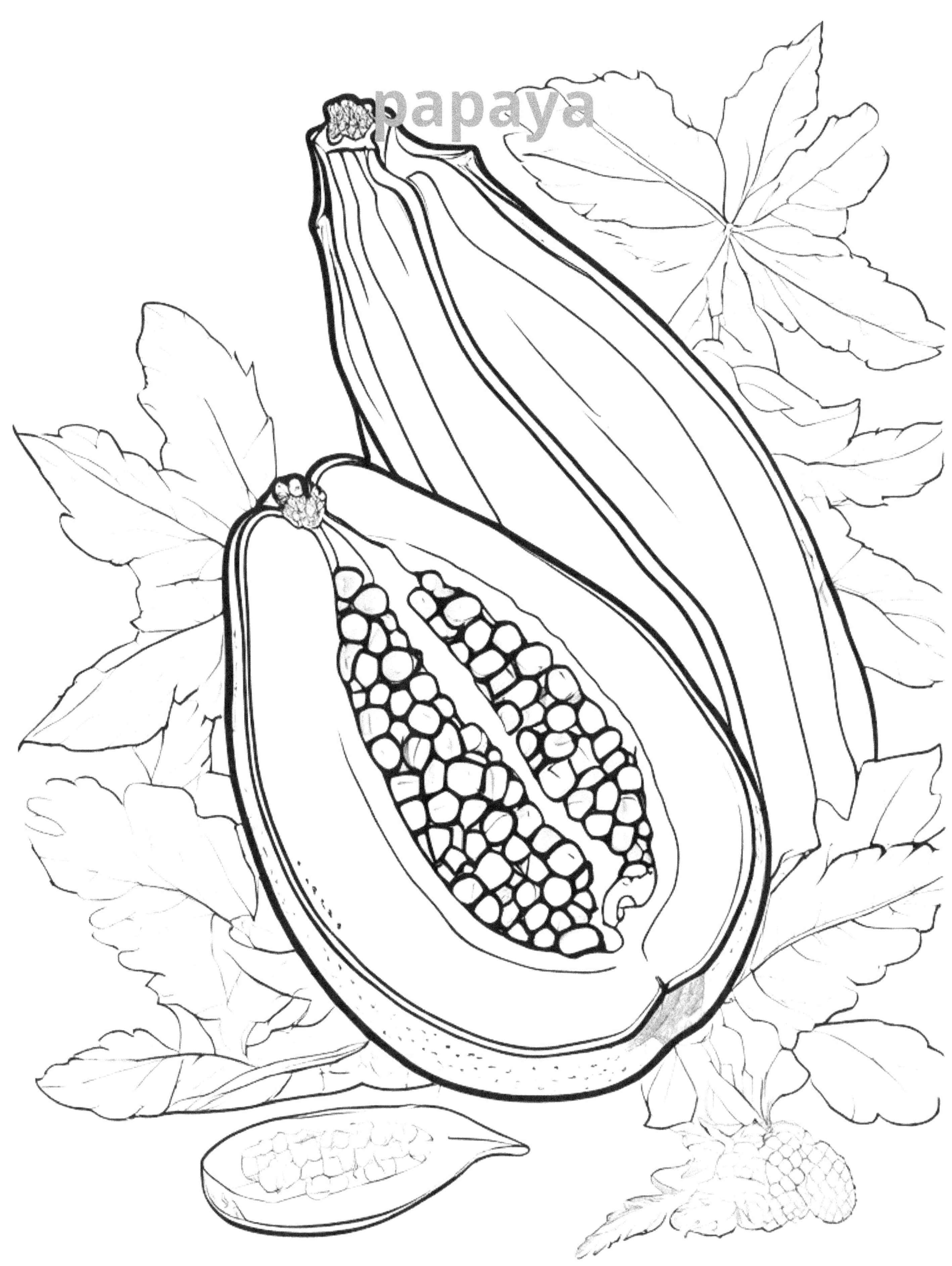
papaya

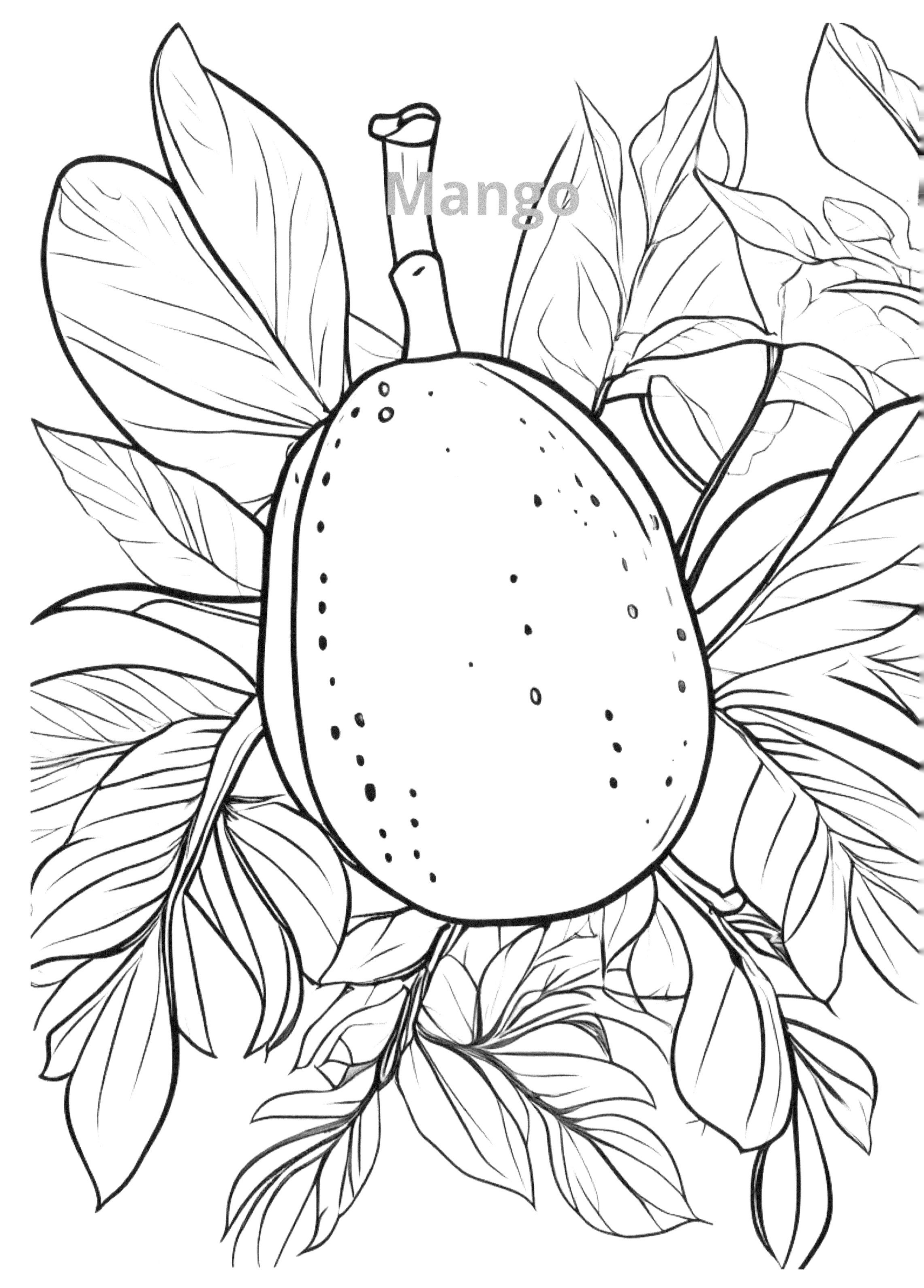
Mango

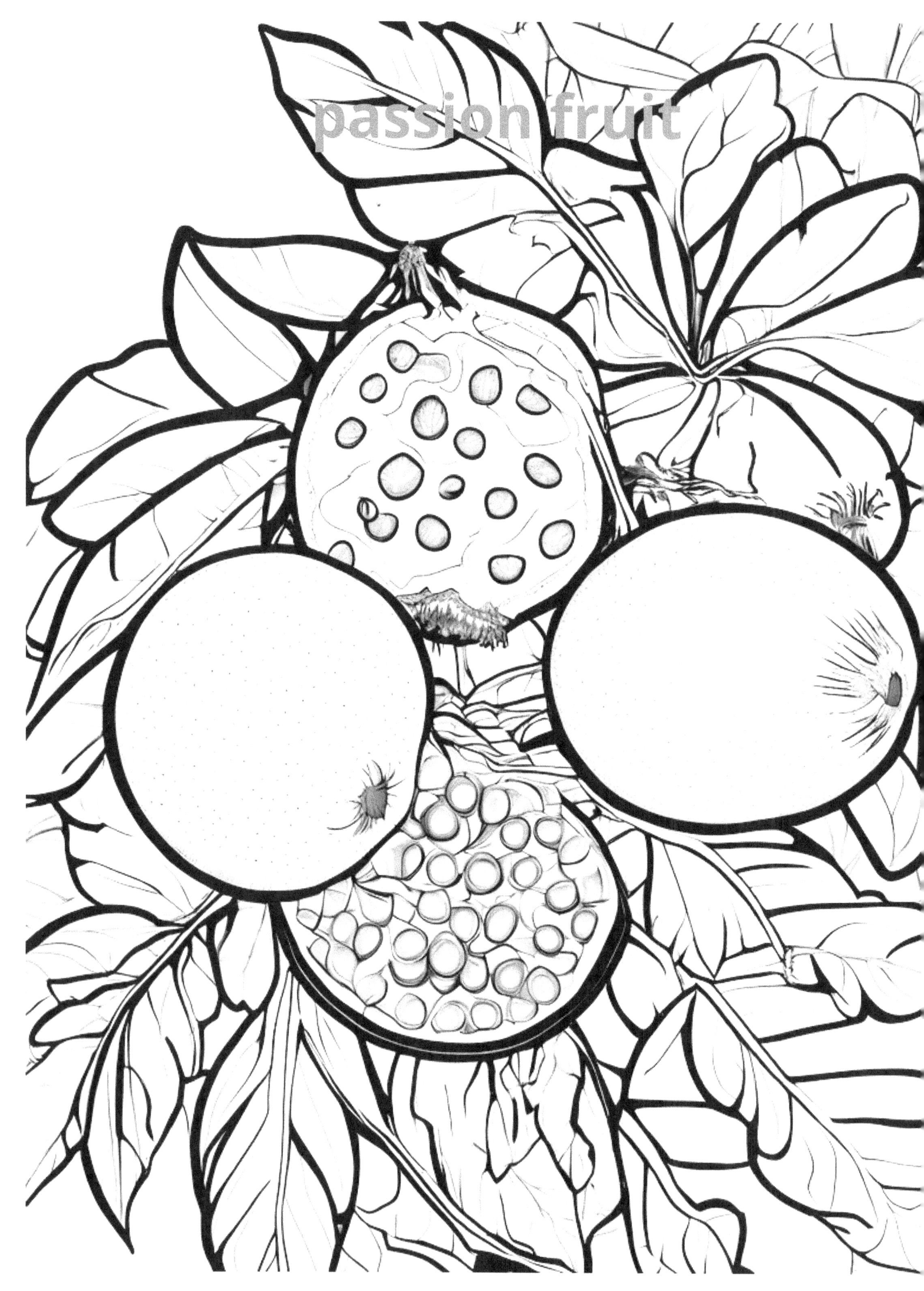
passion fruit

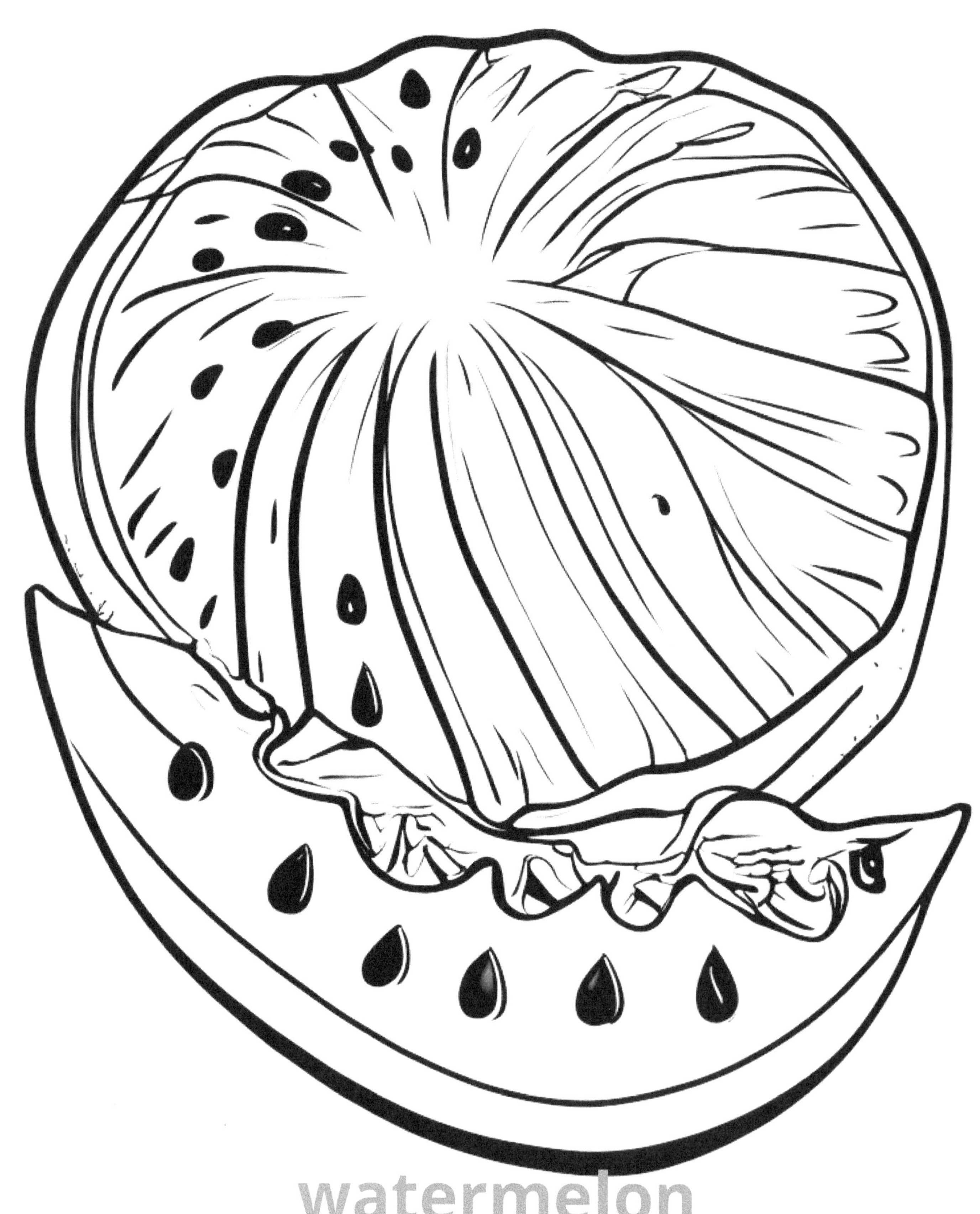
watermelon

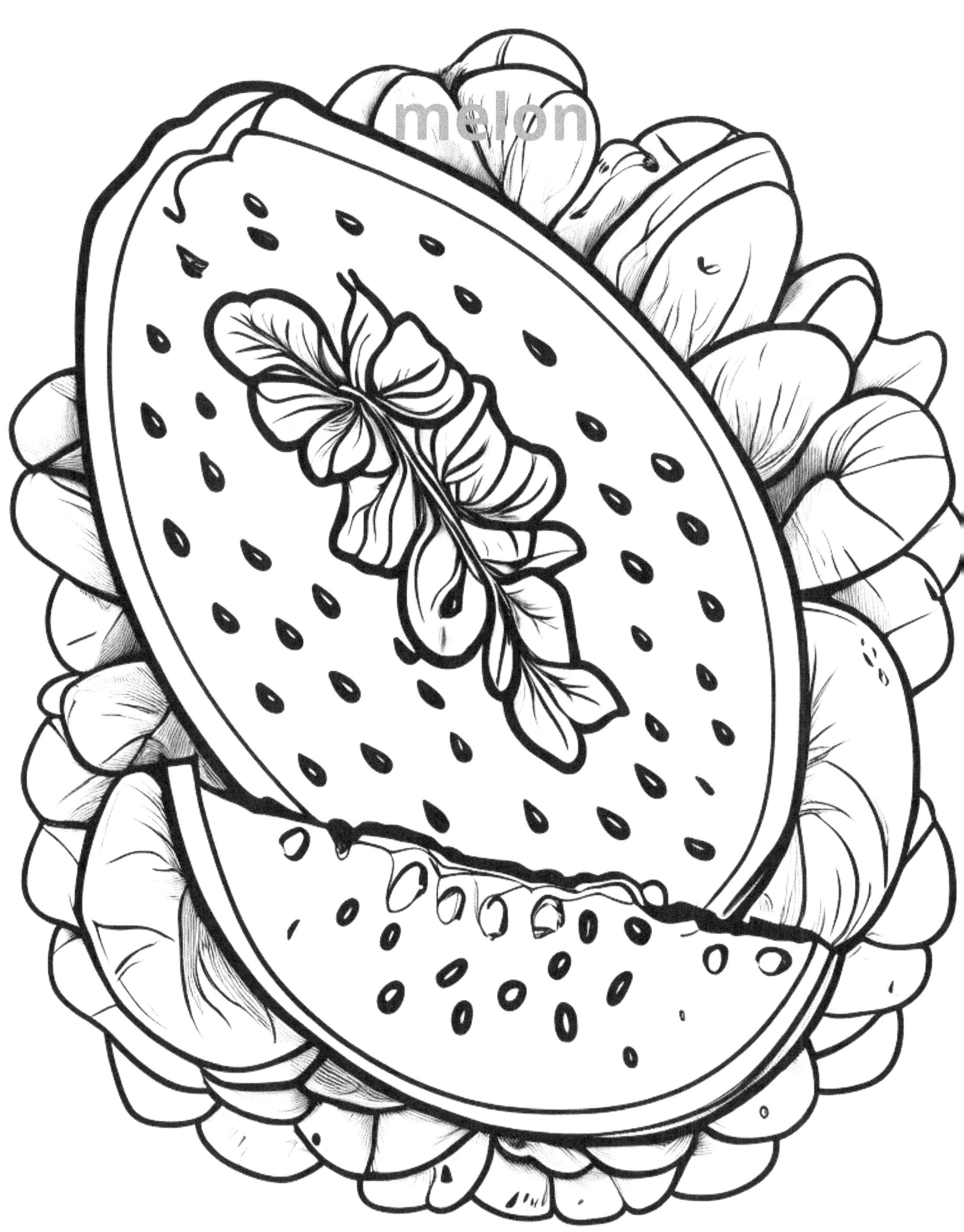
melon

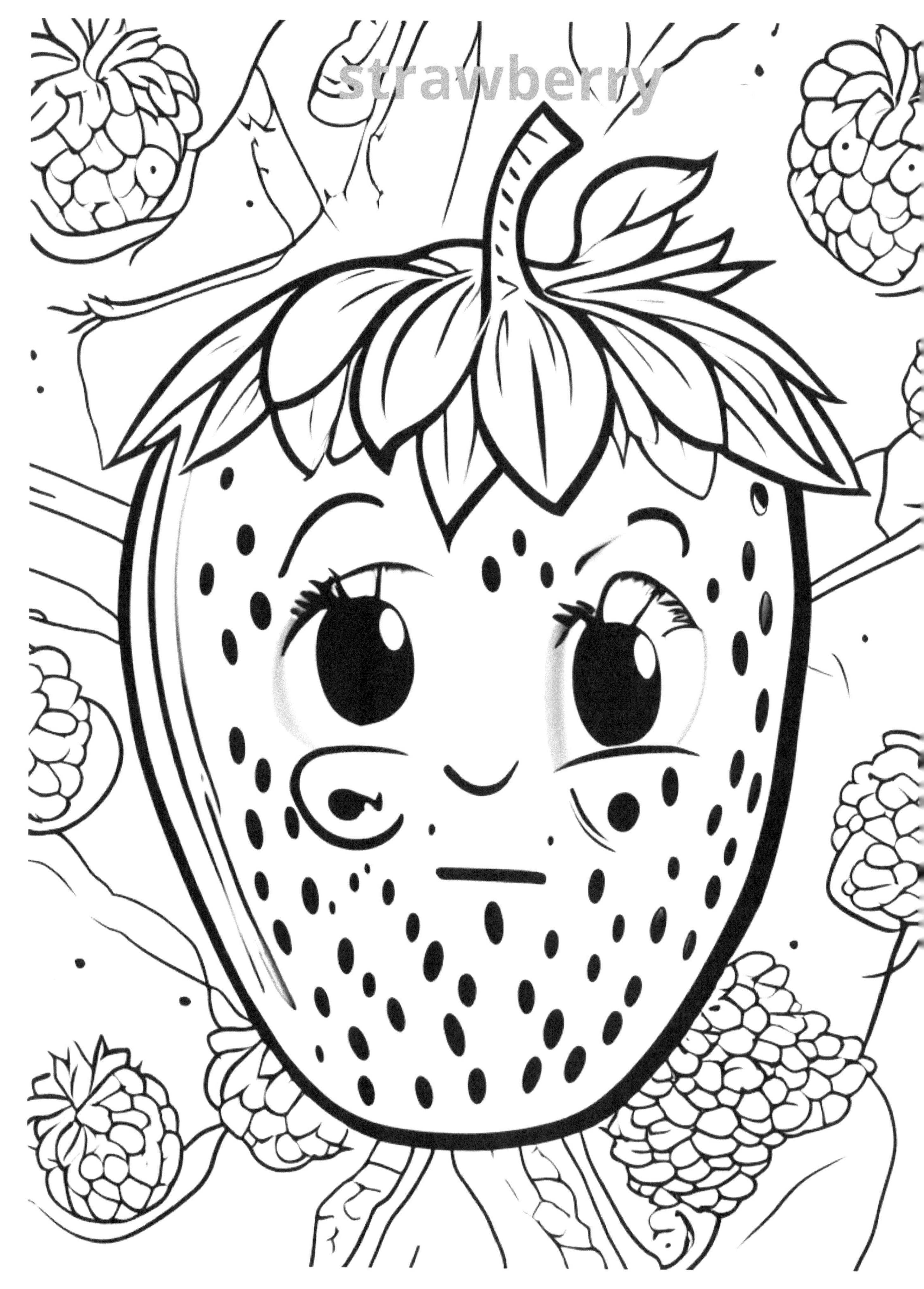

strawberry

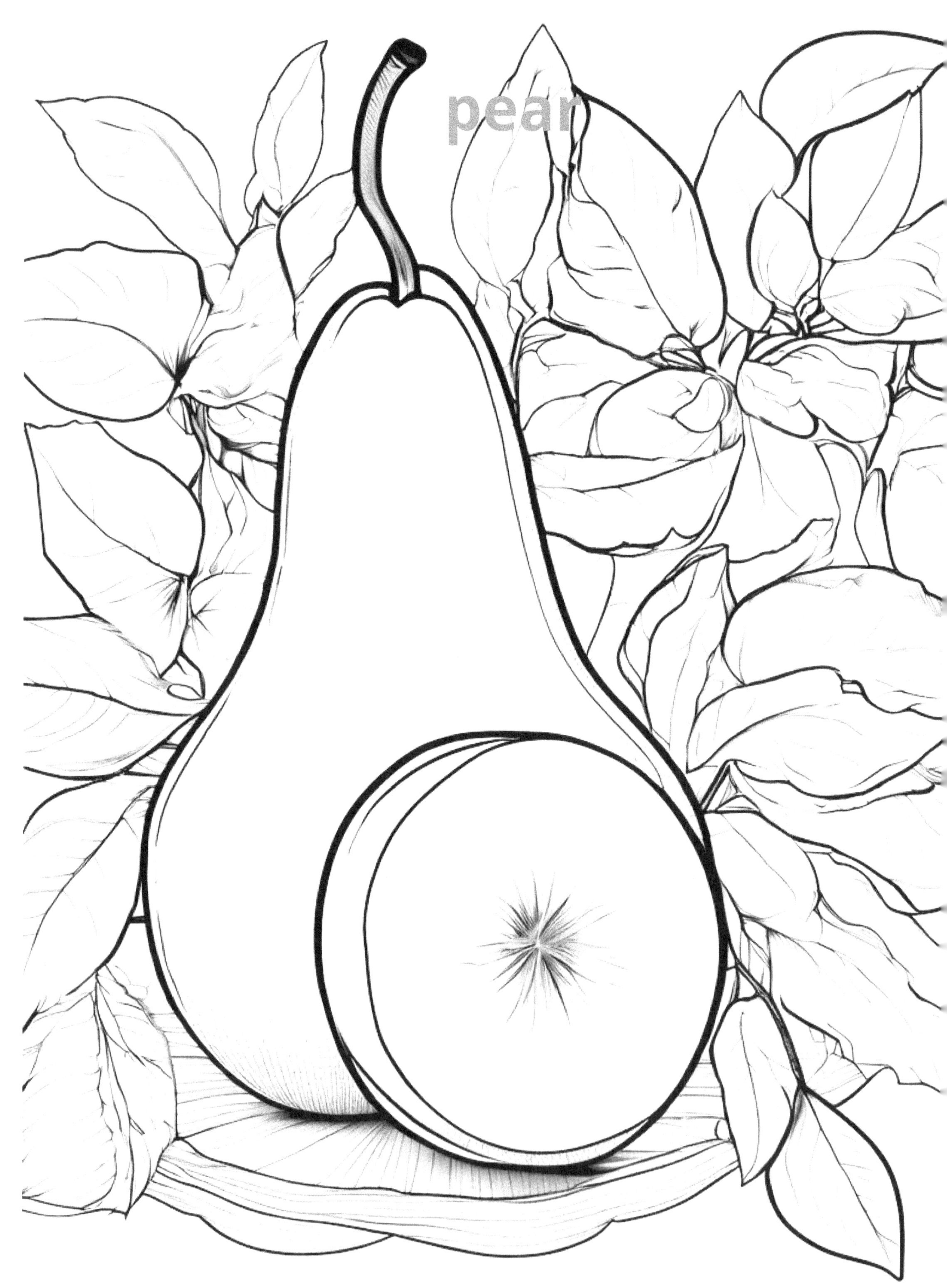
pear

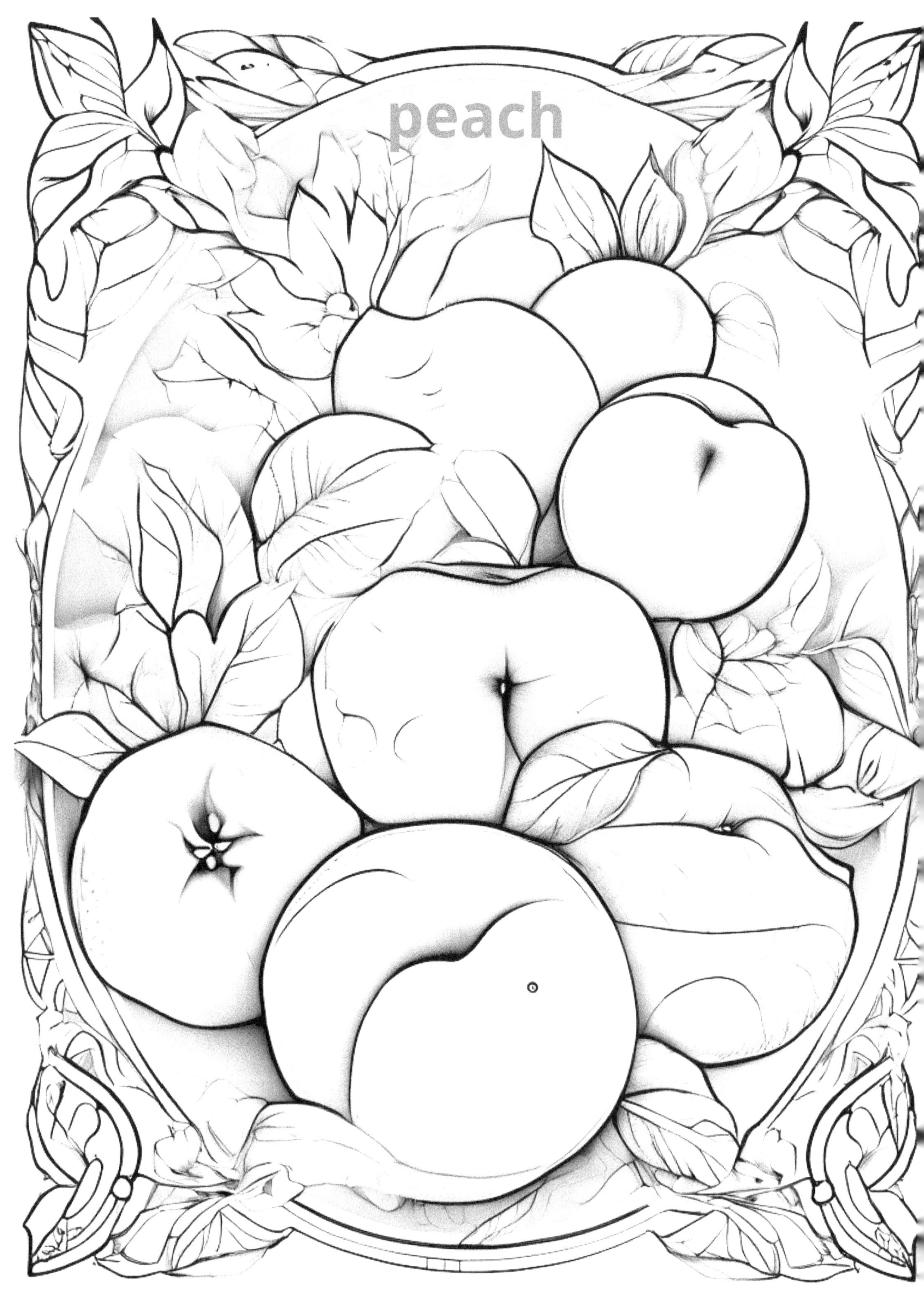
peach
peach

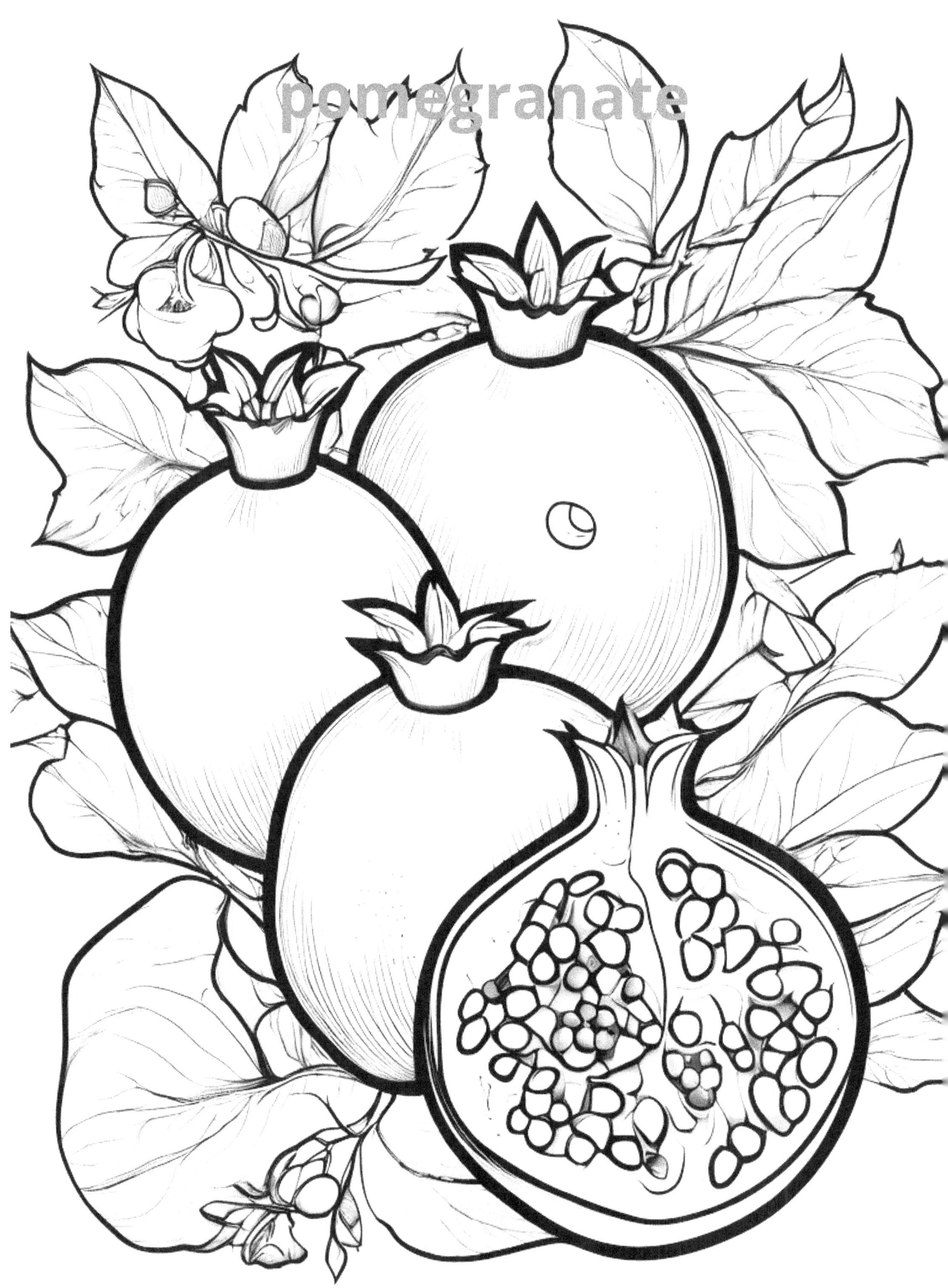
pomegranate

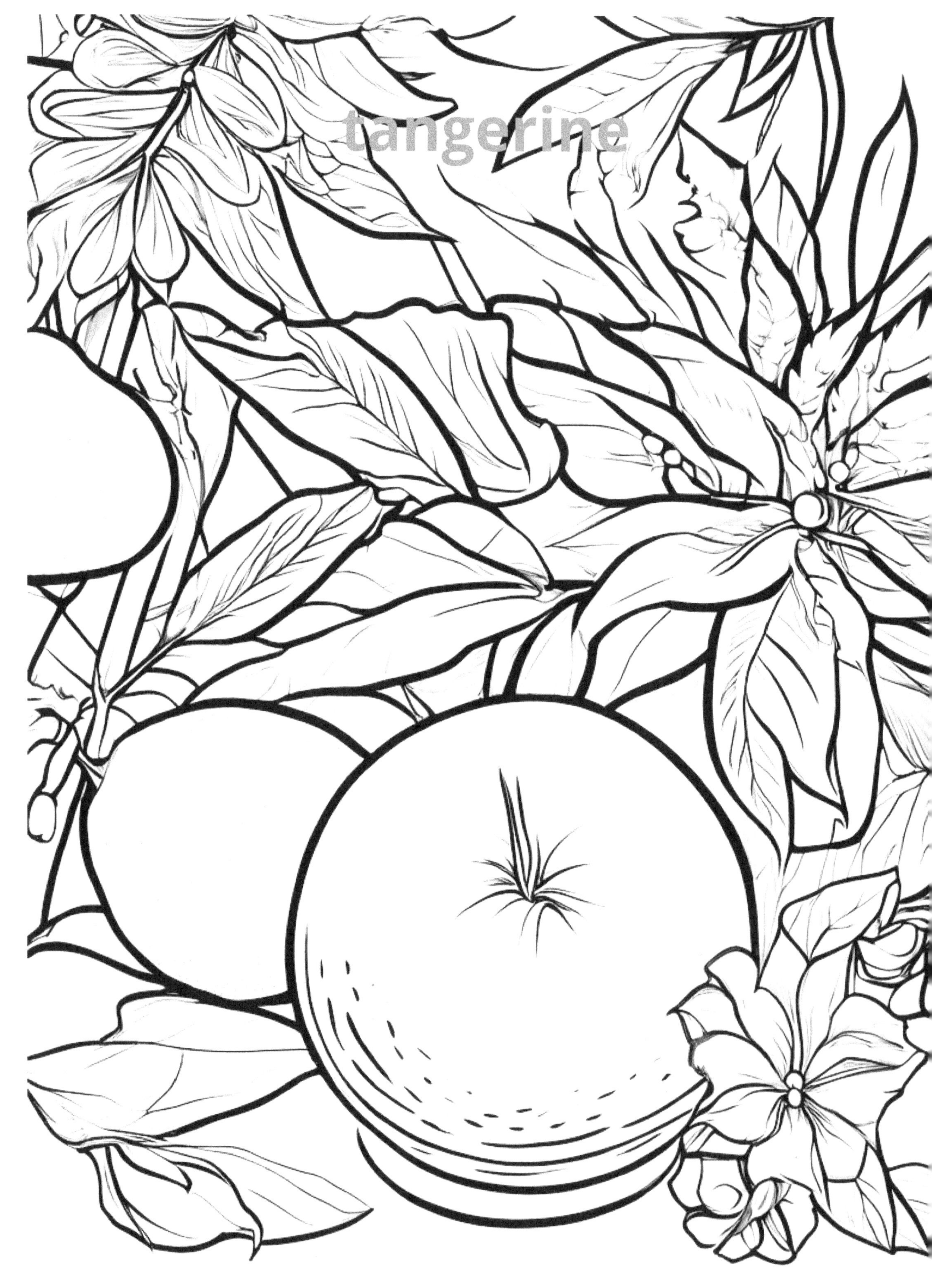
tangerine

www.ingramcontent.com/pod-product-compliance
Lightning Source LLC
Chambersburg PA
CBHW080233260726
48658CB00008B/3080